Dedication

This book is dedicated to the concept of Authentic Leadership. Leadership is both genealogical and situational. All individuals are born with dormant leadership genes. Some leaders have innate leadership skills. Good examples are Martin Luther King and John F. Kennedy. Others become leaders in response to situations in everyday life. This is exemplified by the single mother who must support her family without the assistance of a partner.

Authentic leaders develop a mindset to achieve a fulfilling and successful life. They continually strive to become the best version of themselves and empower others to become the best version of themselves. They prod others to achieve the optimal balance of personal and professional goals and recognize that we are all citizens of one world, and they realize the importance of human connectedness. *Differencia* addresses these issues surrounding authentic leadership.

DIFFERENCIA

CREATING A CULTURE FOR SUCCESSFUL DECISION-MAKING

Robert Cuomo Ph.D.

John DiCicco Ph.D.

ISBN: 979-8-218-23208-5

This is a work of fiction. Unless otherwise indicated, all the names, characters, businesses, places, events, medical assessments, outcomes, and incidents in this book are either the product of the author's imagination, research, or used in a fictitious manner. Any resemblance to actual persons, living or dead, or actual events is purely coincidental.

Table of Contents

Robert J. Cuomo

Dr. Robert J. Cuomo is President of *The Cuomo Consulting Group*, a firm which specializes in executive leadership, coaching, and helping individuals make effective career decisions. Dr. Cuomo is the former Dean of the Girard School of Business at Merrimack College in North Andover, MA and Founding Dean of the School of Business at Dean College in Franklin, MA. He earned a Ph. D. in Economics from Boston College in 1977 and graduated summa cum laude from Merrimack College. He has an extensive professional network, has held senior management positions in the corporate, consulting, and higher education industries, and understands effective organizational management and what it takes to be successful in today's rapidly changing business world. He has designed and implemented numerous programs to foster executive development, and has been instrumental in building bridges between the academic and business worlds.

Robert J. Cuomo is the Chief Financial Officer of *The Joey Fournier Services*, a 501(c3) organization. The organization provides after-school activities in Lawrence, MA Public Schools. The program focuses on activities that reinforce violence prevention and prosocial skills such as empathy, impulse control, anger management, problem-solving, and conflict resolution.

Dr. Cuomo has provided expert witness testimony before legislative bodies, including the U.S Congress and the Massachusetts Department of Public Utilities. He is frequently interviewed by newspapers and radio stations to provide commentary on leadership and economic issues. He has written columns for the *Eagle Tribune*, appeared regularly on WCAP radio, and has been a frequent guest on the local cable television station.

Dr. Cuomo has taught economics courses at Boston College, Babson College, Merrimack College, Dean College, Lasell University, Cambridge College and the University of Phoenix. These courses have included Industrial Organization, Public Finance, Econometrics, International Trade, Labor Economics, Economic Development, Comparative Economic Systems, Business Ethics and Negotiations.

On a personal note, Dr. Cuomo lives in North Andover and has been married to his wife Donna for 53 years. They have two adult children, Mark and Rachel, both of whom live locally.

John A. DiCicco

Dr. DiCicco taught in the Business Department at Curry College in Milton, MA from 1999-2021. He taught several business- and business-related courses with a specialization in leadership. Since, 2019, Professor DiCicco has been a senior affiliate faculty member at Wentworth Institute of Technology in the School of Management, specializing in communications, project management, marketing, organizational behavior, and leadership.

Dr. DiCicco served as the Campus College Chair of Graduate Business Management Programs at the University of Phoenix, Massachusetts Campuses, from 2007-2014. Between 2014-2016, he also taught Micro and Macro Economics at Dean College in Franklin, MA.

From 1991 to present, Dr. DiCicco has served as the president of Organizational Analysis Systems, a management consulting group located in Brockton, MA, specializing in organizational and leadership consulting and training to upper and middle level managers, in order to be more responsible leaders in their respective fields.

DiCicco has authored or coauthored *Leadership is a Choice, The Leadership Gene,* and *The Authentic Leader.* Leadership podcasts and newsletters can be found on theauthenticleadercd.com. He can be contacted at johnoasi@comcast.net.

Dr. DiCicco earned his Ph.D. in Higher Education Administration and Professional Development at Capella University in Minneapolis, MN in 2001. He has been happily married to his wife of 43 years, Gale, and has an adult son Eric. All reside in Brockton, MA.

Foreword

By Jordan Rich

Throughout our history, the human experience has been best conveyed through story. From crude cave drawings at the dawn of it all to modern day novels, films and teleplays, the most effective way to reach and impact people is through the sharing of stories. Seeing ourselves, with our various triumphs and failures, portrayed by well-drawn characters who come to life on the page or screen is a time-tested way to convey ideas and emotion. Want proof? Read Shakespeare, Aesop, scribes of The Bible to name just a few.

This communication of ideas through story is the route taken by my two friends, skilled professors and Ph.D. holders, John DiCicco and Bob Cuomo, in their series of books promoting their concept of Authentic Leadership. Now with *Differencia*, we get to follow the exploits of Josh and Lynn, now in their forties, as they face modern day challenges as responsible leaders.

There are unplanned pitfalls, both professional and personal. Our two protagonists wrestle with realistic issues of transparence and loyalty. Like the previous editions, there is struggle and uncertainty. But the characters learn to further grow into ethical, people of character as they better understand and adapt to more authentic modes of leadership.

John and Bob have worked as academics as well as private sector consultants. As men of a certain age, they have the benefit of seeing a lot of leadership testing scenarios play out in the classroom, Boardroom, and job site. Readers will find themselves caring for the characters in this book, and it is easy to understand why. John and Bob care deeply for their protagonists, and through the arc of their story set them on the path to a good outcome.

I hope you enjoy the book, learn from it, and be inspired to share your own story. You just might motivate others to be better leaders.

Differencia, the sophomore effort of Dr's John A. DiCicco and Robert Cuomo is anything but sophomoric. The book comprises yet another step in their very prescient effort to make us, the leaders in business and society, consider our actions when stewarding our businesses. There is a reason the Startup Rutland Business Incubator is partnered with The Authentic Leader. Innovation companies now more than ever before need to ensure they are delivering value to their employees, their communities, their stakeholders. To leave one or more out in favor of another is to sail a skiff made of paper upon a sea of greed and indulgence. We must do better and this book, this program is an excellent start.

Scott M. Graves, *Director*
Startup Rutland
Rutland, VT, USA

Differencia, and its prequel, *The Authentic Leader*, use creative storytelling and thought-provoking questions to get the reader to live the process of effective decision-making in both professional and personal situations. The books emphasize that every decision you make impacts yourself and others in different ways. The authors further highlight the fact that there are opportunity costs associated with each decision you make, and these costs must always be considered when making your decisions. As a business professional and teacher, I appreciate how these books focus in on the leadership factors that are a critical component to achieve success.

Bruce Share, *Managing Director and Cash Flow Solutionist*™
Share Business Growth Strategies, LLC

Leadership gurus Drs. Cuomo and DiCicco have continued their excellent canon in their newest book *Differencia*, an ongoing biographical analysis of a young professional couple's development and use of leadership awareness. The doctors' style is not only compelling and interesting to read, but each section is followed by reflective questions and lessons, conveying the authors' own long experience in the management dimension. Their skill in breaking down complex business and interpersonal issues into basic leadership qualities is remarkable. After forty-plus years of business experience and teaching, I consider this 'required reading.'

Alan S. Adams, *Asst. Professor of Finance*
Sanders School of Business
Dean College, Franklin, MA

Book Narrative for Flashbacks

The purpose of this narrative is to identify and outline the characters built in the book, *The Authentic Leader*. Additionally, the narrative will provide insight as to the rationale of the evolution of the characters emerging from *The Authentic Leader* into this new book, *Differencia*.

There are many references in *Differencia* that relate to *The Authentic Leader*, which will be characterized as *"flashbacks"* by the characters in *Differencia*. What is to follow in this narrative will be a chapter-by-chapter reference to *The Authentic Leader*, the first book written by co-authors, John DiCicco Ph.D., and Robert Cuomo, PhD, on leadership. We hope this narrative will be helpful in bridging the two books together for clarity and understanding of the development and evolution of Josh Keating and Dr. Lynn Ann Marconi, the main characters in the book.

Brief Summary of *"The Authentic Leader"* quoted in this book:

Chapter 1: There is reference made to Dr. Fringe, a former Board Chair of the predecessor to Differencia, Medical Solutions, Inc., that is explained in the book, *The Authentic Leader*. Dr. Samantha Fringe was involved in a scandal at Medical Solutions, Inc. that almost brought the entire company into foreclosure, in which thousands of employees would have been laid off because of her greed and contempt for the hard-working people of the company.

The goal of Lynn Ann Marconi and Josh Keating was to find a way to get by the scandal and keep the company going. Mary Wilson was the daughter of Joan Wilson and best friends with Lynn and Josh's daughter, Jessica.

Lynn and Josh began their relationship strictly as business associates, and eventually turned it into a romantic connection, in which they decided to separate their personal lives from business. Both Lynn and Josh became soulmates in body, mind and spirit, and eventually produced a beautiful daughter who had a measured IQ of 155 at age six. Jessica has also been diagnosed with Attention-Deficit/Hyperactivity Disorder (ADHD).

Chapter 2: In this chapter, there is more detail about Dr. Fringe, a former employee of Medical Solutions, Inc. who had lost her license because of the scandal. She lost her ability to practice as a scientist in the medical field and her credentialing to do scientific research. Unfortunately, the loss was to the whole pharmaceutical industry. Dr. Fringe was a brilliant scientist and she lost everything due to greed and misuse of power. As the company Differencia evolves in this book, you will see her name surfacing as the narrative continues.

On October 1st, 2021, the Board of Directors of Medical Solutions, Inc. approved Lynn and Josh as Co-CEOs. Under this arrangement, they would hold mutual responsibility for Medical Solutions' operations domestically and globally, overseeing the job functions of over eleven thousand employees.

Differencia created a new Board Chair who was chosen by unanimous consent by the Board members who had remained, transitioning themselves from Medical Solutions, Inc. to Differencia. These remaining Board members were not involved in the scandal, under the leadership of Dr. Fringe at that time. The new Board named Dr. Bonny Mulcahy as their new Board Chair. She is a third-generation immigrant who paid her way through medical school to become a research scientist and help those who could not help themselves, heal from dreaded diseases and get the medical attention they needed to sustain themselves.

Many of those who were afflicted with these dreaded diseases could not afford the medicine, and ultimately perished before expected longevity calculations for their genders. Dr. Mulcahy had worked for Medical Solutions, Inc. for over thirteen years. The scandal that was created and orchestrated by Dr. Fringe as Board Chair, almost destroyed a project which would show a potential cure for Parkinson's disease when diagnosed in its early stages, and even slowed down dramatically in later stages.

Dr. Mulcahy replaced Dr. Fringe as Board Director in September 2021. The entire narrative regarding Dr. Mulcahy's evolution from Medical Solutions, Inc. to the new company Differencia, can be found in *The Authentic Leader*, the predecessor to this book.

In *The Authentic Leader*, Lynn reminds Josh how he was able to muster the courage to keep their family together and defend their principles, providing the balance between family and personal life. This is a real eye opener for both Lynn and Josh. Josh had to figure out how to keep his family together, and at the same time take care of a business while his wife was undergoing medical treatment. Purchasing a copy of *The Authentic Leader* will give you all the detail of how this happens.

Chapter 3: This chapter largely discusses the transition and the reorganization from Medical Solutions, Inc. to Differencia. The vision and mission of the new company, Differencia, will be like the principles named in *The Authentic Leader*, holding true to the same basic core values.

In this chapter, Dr. Mulcahy is retained as the Chairperson of the Board of Directors, which voted unanimously to appoint her to that position. Also, be aware that Dr. Mulcahy was the whistleblower on Dr. Samantha Fringe, who was involved in the scandal mentioned above. Lynn, and the remaining members of the Board who were not involved in the scandal with Dr. Fringe, were retained in their Board positions. They also retained Lynn as a Board member.

When the first scandal of Medical Solutions, Inc. took place in 2013, Josh was identified for the first time in a book entitled *The Leadership Gene*, authored by John DiCicco. In this scandal, Josh was identified as a key account manager for a company called Biotech Medical, located in Boston, MA, before he transitioned to Medical Solutions, Inc. in Los Angeles, California. Biotech Medical was developing a drug for ADHD, and was in partnership with Medical Solutions. The ex-Chief Executive Officer, Jonathan Peters of Medical Solutions, Inc. was involved in a scandal with then President and CEO of Biotech Medical, Russel Hampton. As a result of the scandal, both CEOs suffered incredible personal losses and created a criminal record for themselves. They caused much pain and suffering for their employees and colleagues, and damage to their credibility in the pharmaceutical market.

Lynn Marconi, one of the major characters in *The Authentic Leader*, began to ponder some of the facts surrounding the scandal created by Medical Solutions and Biotech Medical. Lynn stated the following: "I believe that we are just beginning a new company with a new vision and mission." Here, she was referencing Differencia. However, she makes it clear that Differencia cannot deny the roots of the core values that came from Biotech Medical and Medical Solutions, having worked in both companies. Lynn goes on to state: "We cannot deny our history, nor can we leave it behind."

Chapter 4: In this chapter, Josh laments that he was unaware of the meditation exercises Lynn must follow through with after her life-threatening experience. Readers would have to read *The Authentic Leader* to find out what those experiences were. However, Josh and Lynn both realized that their lives had been realigned for the better through faith and trust in each other, and how as a family with their daughter, Jessica, they would persevere through all the storms that would come in their future.

One of the travesties of near-death experiences with life-threatening medical issues is the ability to be able to communicate as a family in ways you never did before the experiences took place. Josh, Lynn, and Jessica would need to persevere through their life changes like never before. It was a new beginning or a renaissance from their previous experiences with companies they worked for, such as Medical Solutions that evolved into Differencia.

In this new company, Josh and Lynn are working on a new Parkinson's Disease drug. Here again, another scandal and another setback for this new drug take place. This is like the situation that happened with the ADHD drug when they both worked for different companies. This was a breakthrough that carried over from Medical Solutions to Differencia, and needed to be resurrected in this new company, with a whole new Board, and a whole new mission that retains the core values of the companies both these people had worked for in the past. This is going to be a very tough act to follow for both. This book, *Differencia*, will explain how they get through it all and persevere with an exceptionally brilliant child, two very bright parents, and huge responsibilities on the horizon, given various medical constraints. This will be a challenge for all. They must be able to somehow figure out the work-life balance.

Josh must prove himself here, while Lynn is sidelined for a while. You must really get into this book to see what happens, but also get a flavor for the history it follows. You cannot deny the culture of the past if you are seeking to understand the present culture and its future implications.

Chapters 7-8-9: In Chapters 7-9, Lynn explains her medical condition in more detail. She talks about her neurologist, Dr. Pereira, who has a flair for understanding the human connection, and needs to make some recommendations as to how Lynn needs to persevere going forward. In this chapter, Dr. Pereira gives some very specific instructions to Lynn on how she can mentor Josh while she is sidelined for her medical condition.

Josh needs to understand what type of leader he is going to be, and if he will he be able to make decisions on his own, often without Lynn's assistance. Will he be able to work through Board meetings while balancing his personal life with his professional life? Will he have to make tough decisions that put him at the helm, as the chief officer in charge, often decisions he doesn't like to make?

In Chapter 9, Josh is reminded of his core values and how they can be so manipulated by very bright people like Dr. Fringe, and tarnish his entire career because of his need for power.

Chapters 10-12-13: In Chapter 10, Josh laments when Lynn was in the hospital, and he stopped into a local pharmacy with his daughter Jessica to get a get-well card for Lynn. This was where he first met Mary Wilson, who is now Jessica's best friend in the book Differencia. Here again, you really need to read *The Authentic Leader* to get all the details on how Mary and her mother Joan helped Josh discover what had happened to Lynn, that caused her medical problems.

There were times when Jessica would lash out at her father for treating Mary as if she were some type of common criminal, when she inadvertently sideswiped his car. She brought it out to her father that he only thought about himself and not anyone else.

In Chapter 12, Dr. Mulcahy, who is the Chair of the Board of Directors, lets Josh know in no uncertain terms that he is the CEO, and he is responsible for making decisions in the absence of his life partner, Lynn. He could not depend on Lynn for answers when he ran into a dilemma. Josh knows Lynn would always make the right decisions.

Josh had a habit of getting repeated panic attacks when he was under a lot of stress. He would often break down. He realizes that he could make decisions and stand on his own two feet. He recalls some of the words from Whitney Houston's hit record, "The Greatest Love of All."

In Chapter 13, Lynn and Josh finally tie the knot. Many characters in the narrative of *The Authentic Leader* are invited to the wedding.

Chapters 14-16: In Chapter 14, Josh needs to find a replacement for his former position as Director of Operations, before he is appointed as the CEO for Differencia, along with his wife, Dr. Lynn Ann Marconi. Lynn did finish her Ph.D. in accounting and since has taken on the new title as Co-CEO of the new company, Differencia.

It is true that Differencia inherited the original sin from Medical Solutions and Biotech Medical. However, scandalous Board members were replaced with good, honest people, and the new Board would certainly keep Lynn and Josh accountable to Differencia's core values.

Dr. Gibson, a wealthy Board member, invested her family's money in the new organization. Josh very nicely explains the evolution of the scandal and why they formed this new company.

Chapters 17-19: In Chapter 17, Dr. Mulcahy reminds Josh that his job as CEO is to have investors believe that the new Parkinson's drug will work, based on sound scientific research. She is much less concerned with the Board's conclusions to put the drug on hold until a later date. This conclusion made no sense to Josh.

Josh later finds that the decision to put the drug on hold was for a different reason other than what he thought. You will have to read *The Authentic Leader* to find out the reasons.

Also in Chapter 17, Josh is questioned exhaustively by concerned Board members that certainly challenge his ability to govern in this new organization. They want to know how he will deal with the FDA, existing staffing problems of the company, and most importantly, the rationale for putting the new Parkinson's drug on hold. He has a heated exchange with Lynn, who must tell him the reasons as the narrative continues.

Chapter 19, the final chapter, involves a speech given by Josh Keating to a group of the largest pharmaceutical companies in the world. He laments upon August 2nd, 2021, when the problems began occurring from a typical day to the perfect storm in his life.

Book Introspections

Please be aware that these two books, *The Authentic Leader* and *Differencia*, are not ordinary leadership textbooks. These books are written from the perspective of two educators and administrators in public and private education, who have emerged from the corporate arena in leadership positions to educate our readers about the authenticity and accountability of true leadership.

There is a transparency in this type of leadership that cannot be learned from a template or a fixed set of rules. John DiCicco Ph.D., wrote the narrative setting. Robert Cuomo Ph.D., wrote the Lessons Learned sections following each chapter of both books.

The characters involved in the books invite you to put yourself in the driver's seat, as if you were one of the characters, and ask you what decisions you would make as it relates to your personal and professional lives. You need to be 100% honest with yourself for this to work for you.

These books have been designed to bring out the best version of yourself under the most challenging situations. They will mentor and coach you in the lesson plans on how to survive and find solutions to the problems you face. The books tell you how to be proactive rather than reactive. They give you the consequences of reacting more reflectively. They allow you to think out of the box and challenge your abilities to understand what trust and transparency really do mean, many times in the face of adversity.

Happy Reading!

Bob and John

Introduction

Josh Keating and Dr. Lynn Ann Marconi have entered the middle years of their lives and are focusing on what lies ahead, both personally and professionally. They are returning to a company that has been battered with scandals, deceit, and a damaged reputation on domestic and global platforms.

Josh and Lynn, both in their mid-forties, are individually and jointly financially solvent and easily can take an early retirement. Alternatively, they could try to rebuild Medical Solutions once again into a world-respected icon, as it was many years ago.

Whether you consider yourself a leader or a follower as you read this book, consider this, if nothing else: You are the leader of your destiny. You will make choices that have consequences for you and perhaps those influenced by your choices. It is an economic principle called "opportunity cost." Every decision made, whether large or small, has consequences for those making the decision. You will need to decide if the decision you make is more beneficial than the one you did not make. In Authentic Leadership, risk is always a factor in decision making.

Differencia introduces a new beginning for our main characters. They will learn that Authentic Leadership leads to Authentic Loyalty, which will be tested and demonstrated throughout the narrative.

Readers will discover that Authentic Loyalty is achieved by optimizing the balance of work and personal goals in themselves, their subordinates, and peers. They realize that financial statements and profitability are not an end game in life. They satisfy physiological needs, but do not speak to higher order needs such as character and purpose. Finally, readers will understand that human interaction and connectedness are the key to becoming the best version of themselves.

Take this continued journey with Josh Keating, Lynn Ann Marconi, and their daughter Jessica, in our second book, *Differencia*. Learn the Authentic Loyalty they discover by building character, integrity, and connectedness to themselves and their daughter. Discover how searching for the Authentic Leader takes their subordinates on a journey of self-discovery and reflection on the true meaning of authenticity.

In the beginning, this will be a tough sell to many employees of Medical Solutions. However, in the end, you, the reader, will have to determine if the changes hold up to the opportunity cost of not making them. Whom will it benefit, and why? Will it be worth it to make a difference? Hence, it will lead to discovering a new company name, "Differencia." Read inside without skipping a word or missing a beat, to find out what the name change really means!

John

Chapter 1
Transgression to Transparency

It is a beautiful Sunday morning on March 13th, 2022. Jessica and I have returned from buying our usual Sunday treats comprising sweet rolls, chocolate milk for Jessica, and a large mocha latte for me at Starbucks. Lynn has her usual Earl Gray tea and a veggie egg wrap. It has been just about eight months since the scandal at Medical Solutions. It has taken us all that time to clean up the mess created by Dr. Fringe and a partially corrupt Board of Directors, not to mention a new Parkinson's drug that still has yet to be released for distribution. Additionally, we needed to keep eleven thousand employees motivated and up to speed domestically and abroad.

After breakfast with Jessica and Lynn, I decided to go for a two-mile run around my neighborhood. While I was running, I remember what Lynn said to me just before we decided to take on the world with our new company. Our previous transcripts in the book *The Authentic Leader* ended with Lynn smiling at me in its final chapter.

Lynn responded "Yes, as Co-CEO, I cannot remain as Chair of the Board of Directors. This would be unethical. The Board would have to vote on another Chair. However, I could remain a Board member. I need someone to help me run this Company while it is strategically restructured ethically, so that what happened in 2013 and 2021 never happens again." Lynn continues. "We will no longer have any secrets since we will be working together as one business collaborative and hold strategic objectivity in every decision that we make. We will be one, personally and professionally, and be joined at the hip, for sure. I will mentor you, and you will mentor me. From now on, we will be each other's legacy and make a case for the next Authentic Leader."

After my run, I return to the house, take a shower, and observe Jessica FaceTiming her friend, Mary Wilson. Jessica and Mary have tightly bonded since Mary inadvertently sideswiped my vehicle last August after purchasing a birthday card for her mother, Joan. You can learn the details of how Jessica Marconi-Keating and Mary Anne Wilson bonded by reading *The Authentic Leader*, which served as the precursor to this narrative, continuing our journey in pursuit of authentic leadership.

For purposes of this narrative, I will share with you that Joan Wilson, Mary's mom, and Lynn have become best friends since Lynn's hospital stay, and have shared some interesting statistics about their children. Jessica, who will be six years of age this coming August, is a gifted child who tested at genius levels last year, scoring an IQ equivalent of 155. She had also been diagnosed with ADHD at age three. Mary will be seventeen this coming October and has been diagnosed with ADHD and Dyslexia.

You may ask yourself why Mary and Jessica have bonded so well. How is it that a five-year-old can connect with a sixteen-year-old? What could they possibly have in common? They both have high levels of (EQ) emotional intelligence. They understand and feel for each other, rather than using their intellectual differences to the detriment of human understanding. They use it as a catalyst for collectiveness.

Mary feels a responsibility to protect Jessica because of their age difference. Jessica looks up to Mary as a big sister who is an only child. Mary was adopted by her mother, Joan, a career professional who never married. She adopted Mary from an orphanage in South Korea almost fourteen years ago. Joan had everything. She had money, an illustrious career as a law enforcement officer, and yet something was missing. Joan calls it "her malnourished soul." She needed something more in her life. Something was missing. Hence, Mary came along. Mary and Jessica met by accident, literally. Was their meeting random? Or was it a part of a planned fate for Joan, Mary, Jessica, Lynn, and me? You will have to decide that as this story unfolds.

Time never stands still, and events keep unraveling and evolving. Management talks about experience, expertise, and strategy. It always has an end game. Leadership involves trust, empathy, transparency, humility, understanding, strategic initiatives, planned and unplanned evaluation. Management does not make choices. Leadership is up to you. Authentic leadership will evolve in this book.

You will have an opportunity to evolve into a diverse world that only opens the door to "we" and closes the door to "me." You cannot be diverse by putting yourself at the center of your career through your actions alone. You need to embrace your resources as unlabeled, cherished, and needed.

Does all this seem like a bunch of words right now? Then good, you need to read my story to find out why I live my life every day as if it were my only day on earth to make a difference. You see, the story I am about to tell you is about discovering the leader in me through the eyes of those with whom I interact day in and day out, directly, or indirectly.

I found throughout this story that character, wisdom, understanding, transparency, empathy, compassion, and loyalty cannot be bought. These traits must be developed. Each one of these traits will be tested throughout this storyline. Can you pass the test? Will you find the authentic leader in you? Will you know when you see it? Keep reading and keep evolving. One last thing: if you stop evolving, you will never find your authenticity. Now, on to "Lessons Learned" and Chapter 2.

Lessons Learned

Chapter 1

The narrative begins on March 13th, 2022, about eight months after the scandal at Medical Solutions occurred.

Medical Solutions is restructured to rectify the disruption caused by Dr. Fringe's behavior, the corrupt Board of Directors, and the decision to not release the new Parkinson's drug.

Lynn resigns as Chair of the Board of Directors but remains on the Board.

Lynn and Josh both assume the role of Co-CEO. This will assure complete transparency in both their personal and professional lives with no secrets.

Jessica and Mary Wilson have bonded since Mary accidentally swiped Josh's car last August.

Jessica will be six years old this August and is designated a gifted child, testing at the genius level. Mary Wilson will be seventeen in October.

Both Jessica and Mary have been diagnosed with ADHD and have high emotional intelligence. Jessica looks up to Mary as a big sister. Joan Wilson adopted Mary to achieve a more fulfilling personal life.

Events will evolve in the lives of Josh, Lynn, Jessica, and Mary. Leadership principles will be identified in their actions.

A successful life will require a delicate balance between personal and professional goals.

Leadership traits such as character, wisdom, understanding, transparency, compassion, and loyalty are not all inherent in us but often must be cultivated daily. "The road to success is always under construction." The storyline will allow readers to assess the degree to which the characters are leading a successful life.

A key characteristic of an authentic leader is authentic loyalty. Authentic leaders cultivate loyalty to them from those they are in contact with.

Loyalty can be defined as the unequivocal dedication to a person based upon that person's beliefs.

There are many historical examples of authentic loyalty: loyalty to Lincoln to save the Union; loyalty to Martin Luther King to end slavery; loyalty to the "Green New Deal" to reduce carbon emissions.

Jessica and Mary have great trust with each other. What is this trust based upon? Is it based upon similar personality characteristics? What are your trustworthy relationships based upon? Are they based upon similar personality characteristics? What are these characteristics?

Josh and Lynn have a new relationship as Co-CEO's. They believe that this will establish transparency and trust in their relationship. Given their past, do you believe this will happen? Why or why not? In your career, have you ever been involved in such a relationship? If so, explain that relationship. Are you willing to enter such a relationship in the future? How would you structure it?

Do we have the right to expect loyalty from others or must it be earned?

Do others have the right to expect loyalty from you or must it be earned?

Who are you loyal to in your life? Should you expand the individuals to whom you are loyal? If so, how would you accomplish this?

Who are those who are loyal to you? Why are they loyal to you?

Empathy and compassion are key components of loyalty. Do you have a feeling or understanding for what others are experiencing in their everyday life? As Dale Carnegie states in his classic book *How to Win Friends and Influence People*, "put yourself in the other guy's shoes." How can you increase the empathy you have for others?

Loyalty is driven by trust. Do you trust others? Do you assume that others will be trustworthy with you, or do you expect others to earn your trust?

How can you cultivate more trust from others?

Authentic leaders are transparent and vulnerable, i.e., they mean what they say and say what they mean. They do not equivocate. Their actions are driven by following their core principles. Are you transparent in your dealings with others? If so, how? How can you increase your transparency?

The human connectedness exhibited by authentic leaders is tied to the relationships they have with others. Authentic leaders realize that life is "relational, not transactional." They recognize the goals of others and shape their actions to address the achievement of these goals. How are you "connected" with others?

Key Leadership Qualities Identified

Wisdom - Authentic leaders have a wide variety of life experiences which allow them to help others in dealing with daily challenges. They learn from their mistakes and pass on to others, solutions that have worked for them.

Empathy - Having compassion for what others are going through in their daily lives. This allows authentic leaders to develop tailored advice to others in assisting them to achieve their personal and professional goals.

Loyalty - Being steadfast in supporting others in the achievement of their personal and professional goals, which allows others to become the best version of themselves.

Trust - Cultivate in others the feeling that you have their best interests at heart. In the words of Maya Angelou, "I've learned that people will forget what you've said, people will forget what you did, but people will never forget how you made them feel."

Transparency - Clearly expressing to others one's core principles, i.e., one's moral compass. This is key to relationship building and the development of trust.

Chapter 2
The Board Meeting

It is Friday morning, March 18th, 2022. Lynn and I are scheduled to have a Board meeting at 10:00 AM sharp. This is one of several Board meetings that include new Board members replacing those found in default of their fiduciary agreement with Medical Solutions due to illegal and unethical practices during their tenure. One of those replaced Board members included Dr. Samantha Fringe, the former Board director of Medical Solutions, Inc. Dr. Fringe lost her license to operate as a scientist in the medical field, including her ability to credential researched scientific findings discovered by her peers. A brilliant scientist, she lost everything due to greed and the misuse of power. Expect her name to resurface as this narrative continues.

On October 1st, 2021, the Board of Directors of Medical Solutions, Inc. approved Lynn and me as Co-CEOs. Under this arrangement, we would hold mutual responsibility for all Medical Solutions' operations domestically and globally, overseeing the job functions of over eleven thousand employees.

The new Board chair was chosen by unanimous consent by the remaining Board members. Her name is Dr. Bonnie Mulcahy. She is a third-generation immigrant who worked her way through medical school to become a research scientist and help those who could not help themselves heal from dreaded diseases and get the medicine they needed to sustain themselves. However, many of them cannot afford the medicine and ultimately perished before expected longevity calculations for their genders. Dr. Mulcahy has worked for Medical Solutions for over thirteen years. The Parkinson's project was her baby, and she was not going to let anyone destroy it. Dr. Mulcahy replaced Dr. Fringe as a Board director on September 1st, 2021. Readers can get the full narrative of Dr. Mulcahy in the book entitled *The Authentic Leader*, the predecessor of this book.

Dr. Mulcahy is incredibly credentialed, with a long history of success as a scientist, researcher, and loyalty to her craft and her Company. The Board chose her as their new director because of her strong core values and ethical practices in the field. She has proven to be a strong leader, with a tendency toward altruism, keeping corporate social responsibility at the forefront of her strategic planning for Medical Solutions, in long and short-term planning.

I felt very comfortable with a new Board director who would keep in the forefront the principles on which this company was founded. I learned over time that power and greed can easily take over the most successful enterprises and turn saints into sinners.

Over the past six months, Lynn and I have been trying to figure out how we would implement a fresh new start for Medical Solutions, Inc. Lynn is a terminal degree finance guru and has been able to lift Medical Solutions into becoming a recognized world leader in pharmaceutical research, that has led to the invention and implementation of miracle drugs. Unfortunately several scandals had corrupted this process and had prevented our company and our employees from reaching medical miracles, which might have saved the lives of hundreds of thousands of individuals.

At present, we are on the verge of getting approval for a drug that will slow and maybe even stop the spread of Parkinson's disease. However, there is still a considerable amount of skepticism in getting the drug passed through the FDA, because of the recent scandal involving Dr. Fringe and others that contributed to releasing data that was not accurate to a federal agency that oversees the health and safety of millions of people.

This will become a huge responsibility for Lynn, myself, and for the Board, under the direction of Dr. Mulcahy, to go forward with this project. It will take investing hundreds of millions of dollars in this new venture to slow and eventually cure Parkinson's Disease. We will not be throwing good money after bad because of the recent scandal here at Medical Solutions. Lynn and I will have to work this out with Dr. Mulcahy and her Board.

Today's meeting at 10:00 AM will be focused on a new strategic vision and mission for Medical Solutions, Inc. Lynn and I have been working on this idea for the past several months, since Dr. Mulcahy was appointed director of the Board. Our goal is to make a difference in how we will brand ourselves: as more than just a company; also as a united group of individuals who want to give back to society, something that is going to give them a second chance in life by overcoming the horrible effects of this dreaded disease called Parkinson's that affects the neurological system, both physically and mentally.

This meeting will be a start, a new beginning disconnecting from the terrible demise. It will give hope to so many on the outside, while giving purpose and meaning to so many on the inside of this company. As Lynn had stated previously, we will become a team totally transparent with one another on all business and personal decisions. Lynn will no longer have to hold back on what she does to protect me, and I will do the same. However, we will not be focusing on protecting each other. Rather, we will be focusing on protecting our employees and our customers.

It will not be easy to turn an entire culture 180° in a global environment. We realize that we will have to take a lot of small steps. Each day will be a record of our progress. We will have ups and downs but will always stay on course, once we have our strategy mapped out.

We are about 15 minutes from our Board meeting with Dr. Mulcahy and the BOD. We are ready to suggest a new vision for Medical Solutions, Inc. I am approaching Lynn and ask her, "Lynn, are you nervous?" Lynn looks at me, grabs my hand, and smiles. "Josh, remember what we've been talking about for the past six months?" I give Lynn the most puzzled look. Before I have a chance to say anything, she responds. "Remember Josh, only concentrate on what we are trying to accomplish and not about what you are afraid to say."

Lynn continues. "Remember how you were able to somehow muster the courage to keep our family together, defend your principles and your life partner, and put us all back on track again?" I look at Lynn in disbelief and say to her in a very low tone, the following: "Lynn, it was all you. Remember how you told me you kept it all together while I was just thinking about myself and what I was going through? I had no idea what you were going through." Lynn looks at me, smiles, and softly says to me in an even lower tone while grabbing my hands: "Josh, I didn't want to give you all the credit for saving my butt. How do you think that would make me feel?" Then she winked at me and said, "let's go in and take our seats, wait for the Board to come in. We are going to kill this!" The ten-minute wait for the Board to arrive seemed like an eternity. Finally, Dr. Mulcahy takes her seat at the head of the huge mahogany Boardroom table. Lynn, of course, being both a Board member and Co-CEO, is seated next to me. The remaining associate Board members all take their seats with corresponding nameplates neatly positioned on the Board table in proper order.

Dr. Mulcahy bangs her gavel to formally open the meeting, precisely at 10:00 AM as planned. She opens the meeting with the following prayer, not necessarily directed at any religion, and focused on humanity as new challenges await Medical Solutions, Inc. The prayer is as follows: "Within the depths of human understanding and rationalization, I ask for guidance to heal and reconcile a species of hope and wisdom. I place my faith in medical science and look for the positive forces in the human condition, which emancipate our thoughts, to be shared and viewed as one for the good of all humanity."

Considering the environment I shared at Boston Biotech and Medical Solutions for the past decade-plus, this was a whole new beginning to our past, personally and professionally. It is addressed as present time in which we make changes to affect our collective futures. Lynn and I are about to make our recommendations to the Board of this new company, with the brand-new awakening influenced by medical science in the continued longevity of our species.

I am realizing for the first time that we are no longer victims of our fate; rather we are innovators of our future. It is going to take a lot of hard work using three essential principles that all begin with the letter "P." These essential principles and motivators will be identified as "Preparation, Perseverance and Precision." We will be ready to take on new challenges, but we will do them ethically. We will work hard. We will dot every "I" and cross every "T."

Dr. Mulcahy asked for a vote from the Board approving the minutes of the last meeting. The Board approved the minutes unanimously. She looks at the agenda for today's meeting, which also has been distributed to all the Board members. This is the time for Lynn and me to shine. We are now ready to present our strategic mission, to go forward with the reorganization of Medical Solutions, Inc. However, we need to start with our vision. Wish us luck!!

Lynn stands up and addresses the Board as follows: "Dr. Mulcahy and fellow Board members. Josh and I humbly stand before you and present our vision for this new company. Over the past eight months, we have experienced many challenges and much turmoil within our organization. We were inundated with falsehoods about our products and services. We have made mistakes. We acknowledge these mistakes and have learned tremendously by making them." There was a long pause, and you could hear a pin drop. Lynn grabs a glass of water and takes two small sips, then returns to her speech.

"I would be remiss if I did not share with you today that I, too made some serious mistakes along the way and have learned from them as well. If nothing else, my experiences have taught me that our humanity is what makes us whole, and with our courage to go forward, these learned experiences will bring us anew. Josh and I, as Co-CEOs of Medical Solutions, Inc. have decided, with your preapproval, to rename our organization, Differencia, meaning 'to make a difference' in the Latin language. I ask you now to formally adopt this new name for our company with a vote, hopefully by unanimous consent."

The vote was taken and unanimously approved by all the Board members, to rename Medical Solutions, Inc., "Differencia." The name will become official on April 1st, 2022. All stationery, documents, business cards, billboards, and posters will share the new name. All medical products and anything affiliated or associated with the new company will share its new name.

In preparation for our next Board meeting, we will be working on a new vision statement for Differencia. Next, we will be working on a mission statement. The dynamics of the vision and mission will be focused on leadership principles and good business practices. The plan from a technical medical perspective will not be recorded in this narrative. This narrative will only record the strategic human resource plan for this new company. The rationale for this narrative being written in this manner is to focus on leadership principles only, that uncover two basic mandates, "Authentic Leadership" and "Authentic Loyalty." Next, move on to Chapter 3 after reviewing Lessons Learned from this chapter.

Lessons Learned

Chapter 2

Lynn and Josh are preparing for the first Board meeting of the new Company. They have been approved as Co-CEOs of the new Company.

Several Board members of the old Company, including Dr. Samantha Fringe, have been replaced because of their unethical practices. Dr. Bonnie Mulcahy, the "whistleblower" who exposed the corrupt practices of some of the old Board members, is appointed new Board Chair.

Dr. Mulcahy is a research scientist who has dedicated her life to helping those afflicted by deadly diseases and making curative medicines available to them.

Dr. Mulcahy was chosen as the new Board Chair because of her strong core values and altruism, by keeping corporate social responsibility as the cornerstone of strategic planning for the new Company.

Lynn and Josh are committed to getting considerable funding for getting the new Parkinson's drug approved by the FDA. They drive the actions of the new Company.

The purpose of the first meeting of the new Board was to make it transparent that the protection of the Company's employees and customers will be top priority.

Lynn and Josh bolster each other as they are about to enter the meeting.

Dr. Mulcahy opens the meeting with a prayer affirming the Company's commitment to serving humanity.

Josh asserts the Company's commitment to Patience, Perseverance, and Precision.

Josh and Lynn present their vision for the new Company to the Board. Their commitment to humanity is reflected in the new company name "Differencia," Latin for "to make a difference."

Differencia's vision and mission statements will be focused on leadership principles and good business practices.

The focus of Differencia will be to analyze the leadership principles identified in "Authentic Leadership "and "Authentic Loyalty" and the relationship between the two concepts.

Questions to Ponder

Should the new Board members be vetted before they are appointed? If so, what criteria should be used to screen them?

Have you ever been involved with an organization that conducted unethical business practices? If so, how did the organization react? Was it partial or total acceptance?

Is Dr. Bonnie Mulcahy an excellent choice for new Board Chair? Why or why not?

Dr. Mulcahy is devoted to "situational ethics," which are based on the golden rule "love your neighbor as yourself," which means putting others before yourself.

Do you think Dr. Mulcahy is sincere in her stated commitment to situational ethics? Why or why not? Do you think her commitment to corporate social responsibility will remain steadfast in the long-run, or is it possible that her allegiance might waver?

Josh asserts that "We are innovators of our future" and are driven by "Preparation, Perseverance and Precision." What do each of these principles mean to you? Please define them. Do you agree that these are essential leadership qualities? Why or why not?

Josh and Lynn admit that they made mistakes.

Do you believe in situational ethics? Why or why not?

Josh and Lynn's ability to position the new Company for success will depend upon Dr. Mulcahy's leadership. What leadership qualities will Dr. Mulcahy need to develop to provide effective leadership? Explain. Based upon what you know so far, what insights do you have on this?

It is often said that "Past behavior is the best predictor of future behavior." Given Josh and Lynn's past behavior, do you think they will remain committed to corporate social responsibility as opposed to self-aggrandizement?

Josh and Lynn admit that they made several mistakes in their past roles at Medical Solutions and that they have learned from these mistakes. What mistakes have you made in your career and what did you learn from them? Did this lead to new behavior patterns?

Do you agree with the decision to name the new Company Differencia? Why or why not? Is this name consistent with the Company's mission of corporate social responsibility? Why or why not?

Please compose a mission and vision statement for the new Company. Be sure that these statements clearly articulate the Company's goals.

Key Leadership Qualities Identified

Dedication - The unwavering commitment to achieving fulfillment of a goal. A good example is the goal of the Alzheimer's Association to reduce or eliminate the causes of cognitive mental decline.

Situational Ethics - Love your neighbor as yourself, which is putting others before yourself. It requires personal sacrifice to achieve an altruistic goal.

Learning from Mistakes - Mistakes are viewed as learning opportunities, which allow us to approach future challenges more effectively.

Preparation - Developing strategies to deal with future contingencies. Having multiple approaches to deal with uncertain outcomes.

Perseverance - The continued effort to achieve something despite difficulties, failure, or opposition. An excellent example is that of Franklin D. Roosevelt, who despite the obstacle of polio, was elected four times as President of the United States.

Precision - Remaining laser-focused in the pursuit of long-term goals. Not allowing sporadic events to drive decision-making.

Mission Statement - Why an organization exists; what its overall goal is, and the kinds of products or services it provides. Tesla's mission statement is "to accelerate the world's transition to sustainable energy". Jet Blue's mission statement is to "inspire humanity both in the air and on the ground."

Vision Statement - It is a look into a company's future or what its overarching vision is. It is a brand looking to the future. Disney's vision statement is "to make people happy." Google's vision statement is "to provide access to the world's information in one click."

Differencia - To make a difference in the world, advancing the interests of humanity through actions, which place altruism above individual self-gain. The Parkinson's Foundation is an excellent example.

Chapter 3
The Strategic Vision

Over the past several weeks, Lynn and I have been working on a new vision statement for our new company, Differencia. I like the way the name sounds, but more, its meaning. We are making a difference by creating a new vision for a new enterprise. The work we're doing certainly isn't new. We are still in the medical-pharmaceutical field. So, what needs to change? I keep asking myself the same question repeatedly.

How will the name change affect our profits? How will we treat our customers, and how will they respond to us? Will we be able to satisfy the demands of our shareholders and other companies we do business with here, year in and year out? The name change is as important as driving our new strategic mission. We are not changing for the sake of change. We are changing because we want to make a difference not only in what we do, but how we do what we do, day in and day out. Differencia is more than just making a difference, its meaning in Latin. It reminds us every day what our new vision and strategic plan stands for, every time we enter Differencia's facilities.

This afternoon at 3:00, Lynn, Dr. Mulcahy, and I will begin working on a vision statement presented to the Board of Directors, scheduled for April 22nd, 2022, at 10:00 AM. It is now 11:30 AM on March 21st. Lynn and I decide to go out for a quick lunch and discuss how we will convince Dr. Mulcahy that our vision plan will be suitable for the Board to approve, with her input, of course. Lynn and I take care of any last business matters before leaving the office.

We arrive at a very nice restaurant, "Casa Mia Italiano" 10 minutes from our corporate location in L.A. The traffic at this time of the day is ridiculous. But the quiet time with Lynn is well worth the aggravation of getting through the traffic and finding a parking space. After all, this is Los Angeles.

Lynn and I had made reservations for 1:00 and arrive early at the restaurant. However, the maître d', Roberto, knows us very well. He seats us at our usual location in a quiet, secluded corner in the back of the restaurant, where we can talk quietly and privately without interruption. Many other corporate officers in our company and even our competitors often grab our attention at this very exquisite, high-class restaurant. Roberto does respect our "do not disturb" visible signs and makes sure we have our privacy. We always leave him a very "high class" tip for his services.

Lynn orders a Greek salad with shrimp. I order an old-fashioned cheeseburger with potato fries. The ambient light and deployed sun shining through the stained-glass windows beside our table reflect on the highlights in Lynn's hair. The radiant hues reflecting from her blueish-green eyes make me acknowledge the natural beauty of this woman. At this moment, I feel our souls melting into one entity. I am looking at the mother of my child and see Jessica in her eyes. I see our future and the future of "Differencia" at this moment in time streaming through my being.

Something has come over me, and I don't know or understand what I am feeling. I know that business involves taking risks. All leaders take risks to reach their end games. They have a vision of where they want to be at a specific time and give it a certain value. Usually, that value is measured on a balance sheet assuming the risk is worth taking.

I look at Lynn again, and I see a human being who risked everything to do the right thing. She never asked for credit. She never gave an excuse or an alibi for her mistakes. She always tried to fix her errors and move toward her end goal. She always had a strategy. Why was she different? Why was Jessica different? Was she born with these traits? Did she learn these traits over time? Or was it a combination of both that brought her to this plateau of human understanding and commitment? I don't know any of these answers. My mind is racing as never before, except when I learned Lynn was missing, and I could have lost her. I have this urge to do something different. I need to make a difference in my mind, soul, and body. Lynn is more than a business partner. Differencia is a new company. This is a rebirth for Lynn and me to start over as one. I mean genuinely as one. We need to be a unique entity if we are going to create one together.

Lynn is looking at me as if I have three heads. She asks in a low but concerned voice, "Josh, are you O.K.? Do you need some ice water? Your face is flushed, and you are sweating. Is it too hot in here? We can change our seats." Her voice travels far enough that the couple sitting at the table two feet away quickly turn their heads toward us in a fleeting second of concern.

At this moment in time, I feel no past, no present, and no future. I am suddenly consumed in a nexus of utter complete fulfillment of my calling and purpose, culminating in my forty-three years on the planet. I look into Lynn's eyes again while grabbing her hands softly and gently. My eyes fill with droplets of emotional signals that validate inner joy and gratitude, celebrating that we are now one. Lynn immediately follows suit; her eyes fill with equal droplets of emotional bliss. "Yes, Josh, I will marry you."

I ask her, "Lynn, how did you know what I was going to say to you? What gave it away? I didn't have a ring to give you. I didn't get down on one knee." Lynn looks at me and smiles. "You still don't know much about me, do you? We can make all the arrangements for the wedding soon. I have been waiting for you to 'pop the question' for some time." I look at Lynn and ask her why she didn't tell me. Her response was simple. "If I told you, you wouldn't pop the question, silly."

We immediately begin working on our vision, to prepare for the meeting with Dr. Mulcahy at 3:00 PM. It is already 1:55 PM. Lynn and I need to review what we have accomplished to date on the vision statement. We have reviewed several other mission statements, including the original one drawn up by Medical Solutions, Inc., over 55 years ago:

"Medical Solutions, Inc. is founded on the principles and core values which delineate its vision, to provide quality medicine for those inflicted with serious diseases around the globe."

Lynn and I realize that this vision statement holds to the present day. We also recognize that many things have happened in the 55+ years of Medical Solution's tenure in doing business. This vision statement was written when there were fewer competitors on the outside and fewer conspirators hungry for money and yearning for power on the inside. We know that there have been opportunities to lead the market in new drugs that would promote health and well-being for millions nationally and internationally. We have certain magic within our Company to create miracles for the less fortunate because we employ the world's most gifted and dedicated scientists. These individuals are attracted to us because of what we stand for and do what we do every day. We improve the quality of life through research and the acquisition of huge endowments and donations from our supporters.

Our vision statement needs to reflect our constant endeavor of supporting the original mission of our founders, and embarking on a new vision that will include a drive to make miracle drugs available to everyone who needs our help to sustain their quality of life, wherever and whenever possible.

Lynn and I realize that this is going to be a challenge. The pharmaceutical companies that we work with, including our own, must satisfy market demands, and at the same time, try to keep to our new vision, which will significantly enhance the demographics of our markets domestically and globally.

The remainder of our lunch involved discussing the reorganization of Medical Solutions, Inc. and our new company, Differencia. It will hold true to its name and our new Company vision.

We leave the restaurant and arrive at the corporate headquarters of Differencia at 2:55 PM. We proceed to Dr. Mulcahy's office in the research wing of our company. Dr. Mulcahy is presently the chief research scientist of Differencia and has held the same position for the prior two years with this company when it was Medical Solutions. Dr. Mulcahy is currently the Chairperson of the Board of Directors, which voted unanimously to appoint her as Board Chair. To remind you again, Dr. Mulcahy was hired as an intern for Medical Solutions many years ago. She was also identified as the whistleblower on Dr. Samantha Fringe.

We arrive at Dr. Mulcahy's office. She is already waiting for us with her notebook open. She guides us from her desk to a round mahogany/glass meeting table suitable for three people. After sitting down, she warmly greets us formally and tells us that she has blocked off approximately two hours for our meeting.

Lynn remains silent, and I immediately open the conversation by addressing Dr. Mulcahy as Dr. Fringe. If looks could kill, I would be dead. After observing the expression on Lynn's face at this moment,

I immediately apologize to Dr. Mulcahy. I explain how nervous I am to be attending this meeting with her and my Co-CEO, hopefully future wife, Lynn.

Dr. Mulcahy gives me a very stern and unsettled look. And, as the expression comes around to haunt me, "I am shaking in my boots." Suddenly, Dr. Mulcahy breaks out into hearty laughter and states to me, "No worries, Josh. It happens to the best of us." Then she bounces back and says, "Make sure it never happens again!" She then begins shaking her head and laughing while checking her notes. Lynn joins in the celebration of my daunting stupidity when under pressure.

As Dr. Mulcahy checks her notes, she abruptly looks up at Lynn and me solemnly. "So, what have you guys come up with over the past several months that outlines our new vision? Tell me what you think, and I will tell you what I think of what you think." Dr. Mulcahy pauses for a second or two and grabs our hands. She states in a reflective and meditative manner, "We are in this together to make a difference in how we live our lives and run our company. We seek to heal by trusting the science that backs up our theories. We do not seek, nor will we fall victim, to corporate greed, self-righteousness, and control of others." Lynn and I look at one another as if we had crossed into a utopia or have discovered an oasis in the middle of a desert.

Dr. Mulcahy then continues. "Lynn and Josh, I am not naïve, and I am a realist. However, I believe that the three of us are here today to begin a higher calling of finding the truth about medicine and about the people who make it and distribute it. We have a long journey, and I need to know if you are committed to taking it with me. I look at Dr. Mulcahy, and I nod affirmatively. Lynn follows suit. Dr. Mulcahy responds, "Let's do it then! Now show me what you have so far that I can sell to the Board."

Lynn and I begin going through our notes and tell Dr. Mulcahy that we understand conceptually what we are trying to accomplish, but can't quite put it into words from a leadership perspective. Dr. Mulcahy then looks up at both of us and states, "This is always a hard thing to do. Let's begin by brainstorming together what we are trying to accomplish with this new company. Let's start by figuring out why we changed the name and why I bought your concept. Additionally, why the Board approved everything based on our suggestions."

Lynn responds to Dr. Mulcahy, "Bonnie, why do you think the Board bought your suggestion on the new name?" Dr. Mulcahy responds, "Lynn, many of the remaining and new members of the Board, replacing those who were previously enthralled in personal interests, are demanding answers to why the scandals took place, including the most recent one with Dr. Fringe."

I chime in, "When the first scandal took place in 2013, I transitioned from Biotech Medical of Boston to Medical Solutions in L.A. This was when the scandal on the new ADHD drug developed in a partnership between the two companies. This was the first time the FDA was involved in investigating the scandal Jonathan Peters, then of Medical Solutions, Inc., and Russell Hampton of Biotech Medical, Inc. had created. These ex-CEOs suffered incredible personal losses and made a criminal record for themselves. They caused much pain and suffering for their employees and colleagues, not to mention their credibility in the pharmaceutical market.

Lynn seems uncomfortable and begins to ponder some of the facts surrounding the scandal created by Medical Solutions and Biotech Medical. Lynn chimes in and states the following concern: "I believe that we are just beginning a new company with a new vision and mission. However, we can never deny our roots. For good or for bad, our relationships have been built on our founders in both companies, Biotech Medical, and Medical Solutions, where I have worked. We cannot deny our history, nor can we leave it behind."

Dr. Mulcahy quickly follows up. "If we truly are to become a new company with a new message to the world of medicine and biological research to cure diseases, it is imperative that our new name is a resource built on the principles of our founders. This means that we focus on the founders of Medical Solutions, not Biotech Medical. Differencia cannot be a new entity of a mutual relationship between two companies. However, it can be an evolution of our present company, which separates us from Biotech Medical. Hence, we are starting a new venture. We embrace a new mission. We develop a new strategic plan."

I am now beginning to see the light that exemplifies the genesis and ambivalence of creative thought, which has existed for thousands of years in human existence. The leadership gene that I discovered almost a decade ago is now exuding from every cell in my being. It is beginning to make a difference by participating in this conversation with Dr. Mulcahy and Dr. Marconi.

I do not hold a terminal degree. Yet, I am sitting in a room with two doctors in their respective fields. I am afforded the same courtesy and respect they have earned over the years in their profound professions. I am asking myself at this moment, why is it that leadership doesn't beg for equal credentials to be equally acknowledged and respected? Perhaps relationships are built on commonalities of purpose and mutual goals and the educational tools are used as resources to support those goals strategically. My leadership gene has now defined a clear purpose that I believe is not any component of random events, but rather planned discourse. I earned my way to this table, to this conversation, and I am proud to be a part of it. I genuinely believe that this is what authenticity is all about. It is real people, with real solutions, to real problems that need to be solved.

There are so many diseases in the world, and we can cure those diseases that ultimately destroy the living cells in a human being. We can always figure out how to slow and even cure Parkinson's disease. Our challenges ahead are going to be huge. It will not be enough only to get the drug approved through the FDA. We will also need to find a way for people to afford this drug to save their lives and impending physical and mental debilitation. Our vision needs to be strong and purposeful. However, it also needs to be realistic and comprehensive.

Lynn suddenly gives my arm a nudge and asks me if I was daydreaming. I did want to go on to detailing everything I just explained to you in the paragraphs above. I smiled at Lynn, and we continue with our meeting. Finally, Lynn states that our vision should reflect our new company name. She presents to Dr. Mulcahy what we have been working on over several months. After thousands of drafts, we have only a few words in a few lines to state our vision and hope that she will buy it and sell it to the Board for approval. Lynn slowly takes out a piece of paper and hands copies to Dr. Mulcahy and me.

Differencia Vision: *In a world blessed by nature yet threatened by illness and despair, our vision is to acknowledge and create hope and healing through scientific research and modern technology, to cure debilitating infections of the body and mind.*

Dr. Mulcahy studies the vision statement intently, folds it back up, and hands it back to Lynn. She is wearing a "poker face" and looks at Lynn square in the face without saying a word. I am dumbfounded, to say the least, at how Dr. Mulcahy reacts to our work. Lynn appears startled by Mulcahy's body language and response to what she just read. At this point, I have the urge to lash out in defense of Dr. Mulcahy's reaction to us after all the drafts we did of this vision before we handed it in to her. Why is this so difficult for her to grasp or accept?

After a thirty-second pause, Dr. Mulcahy opens to us. "Lynn and Josh, I am your servant in this company. However, I have great influence over the Board's decision-making. Influence from a leadership perspective is not the same as power and control. I choose to have neither. This is my choice because the previous Board chairs, brilliant scientists, were overtaken by these two vices, leading to scandals that almost destroyed Medical Solutions. This is what justified the rebirth of this organization."

At this point, I need to chime in to Mulcahy. "Dr. Mulcahy, we worked hard over these past several months to do a lot of soul searching. Lynn and I witnessed these scandals and are aware of their damage to the companies we worked for going back almost a decade."

Dr. Mulcahy gives me a long, hard stare and response. "Josh, it is often difficult to separate the forest from the trees. I truly get that. I am afraid your minds are still fixated on what happened and, as they say in a relationship gone bad, on the rebound. You need to think futuristically."

I respond to Mulcahy, "Bonnie, what are you saying? I don't get your point. What does this have to do with our vision?" Dr. Mulcahy chuckles softly. "Josh, it has absolutely nothing to do with it." At this point, my emotions rise, and I feel like a cat playing with a mouse until it has him for dinner. I bounce back in intermittent anger, hearing my voice naturally escalating. Dr. Mulcahy responds calmly. "Josh, only you and your life partner can answer that question. If you can't answer it, all of this is a waste of time. You should go back to work and forget about the name change, the vision, the new strategic mission, etc."

Lynn is startled by my behavior toward Dr. Mulcahy and asks, "Bonnie, how about a dinner break?" Dr. Mulcahy smiles and says, "Before our meeting began, I ordered a couple of pizzas with sodas, and they should be arriving any minute. Let's take a twenty-minute lunch break, and we will still have thirty minutes to chat before we end our meeting today. Does that work?" Lynn and I nod affirmatively, and we leave Mulcahy's office while she checks in for her messages.

Lynn takes me aside during our brief break and asks, "Josh, what is your problem? If you want to be my partner as CEO in this organization, you must start acting the part!" I immediately respond, "What are you talking about, Lynn? She was playing with us in there, and you know it."

Lynn puts her head in her raised hands as her face is reddening rapidly. "Josh, for once in your life, listen to yourself, then listen to me. Josh, you need to get your head out of your butt and act like a professional head of an organization. Dr. Mulcahy was trying to let you know that our vision, although well written, will be a tough sell to the Board."

My response to Lynn does not reflect that attitude. "The Board said they liked our new name and our purpose. Why is she so resistant to what we are doing, saying, writing down?" Lynn bounces back. "Josh, Dr. Mulcahy is not resistant at all. She is trying to make the best case for us, how we put this all together. She can't do that without our input. Now you are going to go back into our meeting. You will be professional, and you will act like a CEO. Do we understand each other, Josh?" I nod affirmatively and grab Lynn's hand as we walk back to the meeting. We both calmly sit down and resume our discussion.

Dr. Mulcahy opens the meeting and abruptly says, "I have some issues going on right now in the company that require my immediate attention. I would like to wrap up for today by saying the following. "The vision is an excellent one. I will be happy to present it to the Board. However, it might be a tough sell." I bounce back to Dr. Mulcahy, respectfully this time. "Dr. Mulcahy, I thought you said the vision statement was excellent and now you say, a tough sell. I'm sorry. I don't understand." Dr. Mulcahy bounces back. "Josh, there is politics in everything we do. Everybody is trying not to upset the stockholders who invest in our products. For good or bad, this is the reality of life. As leaders, we all continue to assess the risk factors in our decisions to go forward.

All our Board members have the same intentions as we go forward. The risk is the mitigating factor when deciding to go forward. I will begin working on the Board to feel how the vote might go. I'll let you know."

Lynn thanks Dr. Mulcahy as we leave her office. Lynn says, "You and me against the world, Josh" as she is holding my hand. Suddenly, while we walk to our car, Dr. Mulcahy comes running out the door yelling, "Stop, you two!" Lynn and I stop in our tracks as Dr. Mulcahy catches her breath as she is running toward us. "Lynn and Josh, I want to congratulate both of you on your upcoming marriage." I turn toward Dr. Mulcahy. "Bonnie, how did you know?" Bonnie's eyes fill up. "A little birdie told me before you left for lunch this afternoon." I think to myself, how is this possible since I didn't tell a soul before I proposed to Lynn today. I respond, "Thank you, Dr. Mulcahy." Dr. Mulcahy returns to her office slowly this time while shaking her head and chuckling. "Lynn, who do you think this little birdie might be?" Lynn responds in a playful tone, "You didn't tell a soul, huh?" I react with negative body language. Lynn responds. "The little birdie is a little munchkin named Jessica."

Lessons Learned

Chapter 3

Josh and Lynn begin to work on a vision statement for Differencia.

They question whether the name change reflects the demands of their shareholders and the companies they do business with.

Lynn and Josh prepare for their meeting with Dr. Mulcahy on presenting their vision statement for the new company. They meet at an upscale restaurant, which provides a quiet setting.

Josh evaluates the pros and cons of risk taking, and questions if Lynn was born with certain leadership traits or whether she developed them.

Josh proposes marriage to Lynn.

Josh and Lynn review several vision statements, including the vision statement that was developed at Medical Solutions.

Differencia's vision statement must reflect the strategic plan for the new company.

Dr. Mulcahy extends her arms to Josh and Lynn as an indication that she is willing to partner with them in leading the new company.

Lynn states that composing a vision statement is a challenging task which will require identifying specifically the goals and objectives of the new company.

Evolution from the original companies, Medical Solutions and Biotech Medical, is difficult because of the scandals both of them were involved in. The new company must remain devoid of the joint relationship between the two.

True leadership is based upon commonality of purpose and not credentials. It requires dedication to a shared strategic vision.

The strategic vision of Differencia is to obtain FDA approval of the Parkinson's breakthrough drug and to make it more affordable to the general population.

Lynn presents to Dr. Mulcahy the proposed vision statement for Differencia: "In a world blessed by nature yet threatened by illness and despair, our vision is to acknowledge and create hope and healing, through scientific research and modern technology, to cure debilitating infection of the body and mind."

Dr. Mulcahy indicates that she will present the proposed vision statement to the Board of Directors. She stresses that she, Lynn, and Josh must look ahead to a new relationship completely devoid of the past.

Josh becomes infuriated with Dr. Mulcahy's remarks and suggests that they abandon the name change, vision, and Strategic Plan for the new Company.

Lynn admonishes Josh for his remarks. She tells him that Dr. Mulcahy was merely suggesting to him that the acceptance of the vision statement for the new company will be a hard sell to the Board.

Dr. Mulcahy indicates that the Board will need assurance that the stockholders who invest in the firm will not be adversely affected by Board decisions. She indicates that she will report back to Lynn and Josh as to what the Board decides.

Dr. Mulcahy congratulates Josh and Lynn on their upcoming marriage.

Questions to Ponder

Do you think it is important to have a **vision** statement for both your personal and professional lives? Why or why not? If so, do you have one? If not, please compose one.

Do you think it is important to have a **mission** statement for both your personal and professional lives? Why or why not? If so, do you have one? If not, please compose one.

What are the key ingredients of a mission statement?

What are the key ingredients of a vision statement?

Do you agree with Differencia's vision statement? Why nor why not? How can it be improved?

Is Josh effective in preparing for his meeting with Dr. Mulcahy? Why or why not? Is he laser-focused in his preparation or is he excessively daydreaming? What should Josh be focused on?

Is Differencia an appropriate name for the new company? Why or why not? Would you have proposed a different name?

Should the main purpose of the new company be to enhance the welfare of stockholders or to promote the public welfare?

Josh believes that the new company will be a new beginning for him and Lynn. Do you think this will happen?

Is carrying forward the vision statement for the previous company, Medical Solutions, a good idea? Why or why not?

Josh enters the meeting with Dr. Mulcahy in an extremely nervous state. Is this a characteristic of a true leader?

Lynn agrees with Dr. Mulcahy that convincing the Differencia Board to adopt the new vision statement will be a challenging task. Do you agree?

Do you agree with Lynn's assessment that the current relationship with the new Board is complicated by the two past scandals that Medical Solutions and Boston Medical engaged in?

Do you believe that Josh and Lynn have a commonality of purpose in the new company?

Do each of us have a leadership gene imbedded in us that is waiting to be activated?

Do you seek out leadership opportunities or do you wait for them to come to you?

Is Josh's defensiveness justified when Dr. Mulcahy stresses that the acceptance of the vision statement by the Board will be a tough sell?

Do you think that Josh is politically naive in not recognizing Dr. Mulcahy's assessment of the situation?

Many people praise themselves when they say, "I haven't made many mistakes." In my experience, I have found that this is "The biggest mistake." Do you agree with this? I have found that failures are learning opportunities to acquire new knowledge and improve decision-making.

I am a firm believer in BHAGs, "Big, Hairy, Audacious Goals." These are "stretch" goals which challenge our current skill set. Do you have any BHAGs? What are they? Please develop two BHAGs.

Key Leadership Qualities Identified

Strategic Plan - True leaders develop a blueprint they will follow to fulfill their personal and professional goals. They develop contingency plans if circumstances change.

BHAGs - Big, Hairy, Audacious Goals. Authentic leaders aspire to "stretch" goals, i.e., goals which go beyond what their current skill set will allow them to accomplish. This is necessary for self-improvement.

Stockholder Value - Successful corporate executives must strive to maximize stockholder value for the firm to attract new investors and grow. This is necessary for the firm to achieve its vision.

Public Welfare - True business success is accomplished by promoting the common good. This means promoting the interests of the general populace, such as food security and producing lifesaving and pain-relieving medications at an affordable cost.

Commonality of Purpose - The sharing of a vision either by individuals or a business. This is achieved by promoting human connectedness, which focuses on maximizing the public welfare, such as reducing income inequality and accepting gender diversity.

Emotional Intelligence - Authentic leaders recognize that they are part of a social context, i.e., the way in which they interact with others will determine the influence they have on others. This is aptly described "Life is relational, not transactional."

Self-Efficacy - An individual's belief in their capacity to execute behaviors necessary to produce specific performance attainments. Development of self-esteem is necessary to achieve this.

Critical Thinking - The objective analysis and evaluation of an issue to form a judgment. Critical thinkers do not automatically accept a particular view, but ask probing questions to produce a more informed judgment.

Chapter 4
The Vision-The Mission-The Board

It is Friday, April 22nd at 7:00 AM, and Jessica has already been out of bed for half an hour. Lynn and Jessica are doing meditation and reflection exercises before breakfast. Lynn and I will drop Jessica off at school and then proceed to Differencia's corporate offices in downtown Los Angeles.

I was unaware of these meditation exercises until we thought we lost Lynn last year. Our lives have been realigned for the better through our faith and trust in each other as a family. I am much more aware of my surroundings and enjoy my relationship with my family. I never realized how much I was missing all these years, especially since Jessica was born. I learned how little attention I was paying to my daughter, future wife, and life partner.

While Lynn and Jessica are finishing up their meditation exercises, I think I will surprise them with a homemade Spanish omelet, bacon, and some raisin toast. They deserve the best because they are the best. While I am making breakfast, I hear something strange in the dialogue taking place between Lynn and Jessica. One of the verbal exercises that Lynn and Jessica do each day after meditation is called "Finish the sentence." Jessica starts with a phrase, and Lynn finishes the sentence. Conversely, Lynn starts the phrase, and Jessica finishes in a complete sentence. They could end up being questions or declarative sentences. The phrases start very simply and require some imagination and creativity to turn them into a complete sentence. The phrases get increasingly difficult in small incremental steps. They usually do about 5 to 7 of these exercises each morning.

One of these exchanges got my attention, and I don't know why. A common phrase between Jessica and Lynn had to do with the poem/song, "The Itsy Bitsy Spider." In the exchange, Jessica leading the phrase, said, "The itsy-bitsy spider went…." Lynn and Jessica sang this song a thousand times, even when Lynn was in the hospital last year and first communicated with her after being admitted to the ICU for a probable aneurysm, a non-epileptic seizure.

This is what I heard, or didn't hear, that sounded strange to me. I did not hear Lynn's response to Jessica's phrase that would have finished the sentence. There was a hesitancy in Lynn's response to Jessica to complete the phrase. I did hear Jessica say to her mommy, "Please finish the phrase and make it a sentence. Then, we can do another one."

Lynn's response to Jessica was, "Why don't we do another one Jess, and we'll come back to this one." There was silence for about 20 seconds, and Jessica said to Lynn, "I'm tired, mommy. I think I don't want to do any more of these today. Maybe we can do more tomorrow." Of all the months that I have been listening to these two doing their meditation and word phrase exercises, this is a first. Maybe they are a little out of sorts today, and tomorrow is another day.

Today will be a big day for Lynn and me, not discounting the proposed announcement of the new Parkinson's drug in August of last year that never took place. This is a new beginning for both of us. It is more of a Renaissance of our previous existence in Medical Solutions, which evolved into Differencia.

Why does this eavesdropping on Lynn and Jessica bother me? I have no idea. It's just a circumstance of events that resurrect my PTSD from last year's experiences that nearly destroyed our family and the company that we work for. Am I just a little bit paranoid here? I am picking up on a subtle difference in an exchange between Jessica and Lynn, which I should discount as just a circumstance of an event that triggered a negative response to some of my previous life-changing experiences.

Lynn and Jessica are exuberant to find an elegant breakfast already prepared for them. Lynn states, "What a wonderful way to start off the day, Josh! You are so thoughtful to think of me and Jess before we even step foot outside the house." Jessica is all giggly and smiling as she tries to shove enough food to fill a Mack truck into her tiny mouth, getting most of the food on her face. Mentally, she may be at a genius level, but physically she is still five years old and acts like a five-year-old.

We are finally done with breakfast. Lynn places the dishes in the dishwasher and makes sure Jessica is cleaned up and ready to go to school. Lynn volunteers to drive this morning and we should be able to drive Jessica to school and get ourselves to work in plenty of time for our meeting with Dr. Mulcahy, and after that, a meeting with the Board of Directors at 10:00 AM. Everybody is in a great mood this morning, and Lynn and I are as ready as we will ever be to get our new vision statement approved by this Board of Directors, since we last met with Dr. Mulcahy in March. Lynn and I have been preparing to make a presentation strong and persuasive. Dr. Mulcahy has spent the last month talking to Board members individually and collectively, and at luncheons, to convince them that our new vision would be not only acceptable, and rightfully branded to our craft, but also be acceptable to our competitors. We are hopeful they will join us in our efforts to eradicate deadly diseases in the world and find a way to make medicines affordable, to preserve human life to its fullest.

Lynn and I drop Jessica off at school and go on our way to Differencia, to meet with Dr. Mulcahy prior to going into our Board meeting. We should arrive at Dr. Mulcahy's office by 9:15 AM and go over all the major points of our presentation. I observe another strange occurrence this morning associated with Lynn, though. We have driven to our destination corporate building for several years now. We always take a left on Berkeley Street, which is the street prior to the second set of lights where we take a right to enter Medical Solutions Way. This morning, Lynn took a right onto Carmen Way instead of a left onto Berkeley Street, which obviously would bring us to Medical Solutions Way. The problem here is that Lynn did not stop herself from realizing she had taken the wrong turn. I had to tell her. Maybe she was just distracted because of the pressure of going before the Board today.

Taking the wrong turn put us behind about five minutes before getting to work. We finally arrived at Dr. Mulcahy's office at approximately 9:35 AM. Lynn is still a little upset and flustered that she had missed the turn that she had taken for so many years to get to work. I told her there was a lot going on and to calm down and not let it bother her. I told her that right now, we need to focus on getting our priorities straight in meeting with the Board, and rehearse what we're going to say with Dr. Mulcahy as she introduces us again, a month later from the last time we met to announce the name change of our company from Medical Solutions to Differencia.

Our goal here is to justify our new vision statement for the company, which will set the stage for our new mission from a strategic leadership perspective as it relates to our culture and human resources. This is all about our company coming together as an entity that is focused less on the employees' needs and more on the needs of the population which it serves. Without the rite of passage from the Board, the connection between the vision and the mission would remain subtly connected to the structure of the old company, which this new one will replace. Our core values need to be reassessed with the Board, relating to our founders and not to any one or more individuals who have been connected to the old organization and/or those that remain in the new organization as Board members.

We are now ready to enter the huge conference room with the enormously large conference table that was built with strong Maplewood legs and a heavy glass surface. Upon entering our last meeting, we observed all the nametags of the Board members aligned with the proper seating arrangements. Lynn's name tag as well as my name tag were placed at opposite ends of the huge conference table. Dr. Mulcahy was not sitting at the head of the table, but rather was seated in the middle. I expected Dr. Mulcahy to be seated at the head of the table, considering she is Board Chair.

It is 9:58 AM and the Board members take their seats, designated by their nametags on the conference room table. Lynn and I are seated on opposite ends of the table, while Dr. Mulcahy takes her seat in the middle. There is much chatter between the Board members as they compare their notes and agendas.

At exactly 10:00 AM, Dr. Mulcahy strikes her gavel to the table, signaling that the meeting is in session. The room is quiet. Dr. Mulcahy opens the meeting by acknowledging myself and Lynn as the new Co-CEOs of Differencia. A loud round of applause from Board members, old and new, takes place. Immediately, Lynn and I stand up from our seats and thank the Board members for their welcoming applause. The minutes of the last Board meeting are read and unanimously approved by all members.

The first of many agenda items is the review and approval of the new vision statement. The next one is the ratification of the mission statement, once approved. There are several other items on the agenda. However, Lynn and I do not have to be present for them. The Board acknowledges we have a company to run and many items on our agenda need to be addressed by day's end. All the Board members have a copy of the vision statement. Dr. Mulcahy introduces the statement and seeks the Board's consensus. A quick review of the statement by the Board members is asked. The statement is as follows:

Differencia Vision: *In a world blessed by nature yet threatened by illness and despair, our vision is to acknowledge and create hope and healing, through scientific research and modern technology, to cure debilitating infections of the body and mind.*

One of the Board members who remained with the new company asked "This vision statement seems very similar to the vision statement of Medical Solutions. How is it different?" Dr. Mulcahy postures herself and signals Lynn to answer the question. Strangely, Lynn has a blank stare similar to the one she gave when Jonathan Peters, ex-CEO of Medical Solutions, came to a meeting at our house almost nine months ago, to discuss and clear up matters regarding the second scandal involving that company.

It appeared to me, and it was my hope, that Lynn was just processing information and was very meticulous and calculating before giving an answer to the Board member asking the question. However, just like earlier this morning with Jessica, strange things were happening with Lynn that I could not explain. My question is, why is this happening now? Why is this happening when it is our time to shine, once again? I really didn't think I could handle much trauma in that moment; this was not the time for Lynn to bail out on me.

Lynn finally responds to the Board member as tears are streaming down her reddened face. "Please repeat the question. I can't remember it! I don't understand what you are asking me right now." Everyone in the room is gasping in horror and disbelief. Lynn looks at the reactions of everyone in the room and abruptly runs out sobbing uncontrollably. I remain at my seat at the other end of the conference table, trying to process what just happened. Immediately, Dr. Mulcahy excuses herself and leaves the conference room, and attempts to find Lynn. I am left here alone with all the Board members, and my life partner and future wife has left the Boardroom, in turmoil and embarrassment. It is up to me now to make some decisions on the next step. This is my moment in time. I am realizing that I have no one to turn to. I can't turn to Dr. Mulcahy. I can't turn to Lynn. I am sitting in a room full of Board members who are waiting for answers to the vision statement that was presented just five minutes ago for approval.

At this point, I must decide whether or not to walk out of the room, continue with the meeting as planned, act as the CEO of this company, and show the Board I am worthy of the position that I hold. Right now, the answers are within my grasp. My loyalty cannot be to myself. I can't make excuses for other people. I am flashing back to what Lynn said to me after she returned home, and Jonathan left our house. I remember still feeling betrayed by Lynn because she kept things from me, because she was CEO of Medical Solutions. She reminded me that my responsibility was first to the people that entrust their livelihoods to my charge, and I must keep family life and work-life in balance, despite the circumstances, and the consequences.

I take a visual of my surroundings and all eyes are on me. I need to take control now or lose it forever. Every fiber in my being tells me to run out of the conference room and check on Lynn. I realize that Dr. Mulcahy has already left the room looking for Lynn and has not returned. Logically, I must assume that she has found Lynn and is doing what is necessary to keep her stable and get the proper medical care she needs. I must also assess if I am being insensitive to her needs as she should be my number one priority at this time, as my life partner and future wife. I am literally torn between two worlds and the answer is up to me in response to this dilemma.

I will stand up and I will address the Board as a professional and a concerned family member. "Dear Board members, very shortly I will be leaving this meeting and respectfully request that you continue your agenda, based on the unforeseen circumstances you have just witnessed. My responsibility to this organization regarding the agenda item you so graciously allowed to entertain and examine this morning must be postponed to a future date, until more information is available to us on what caused Dr. Marconi's immediate need to leave this meeting. I extend my apologies on behalf of Dr. Marconi, Dr. Mulcahy, and myself, for this abrupt but necessary exit from this meeting. When we obtain more information on Dr. Marconi's situation, we will respond to you in writing, as to the next steps in establishing a vision and mission statement for our new name, reflecting our reorganization of the former Medical Solutions organization. Thank you for your time today."

I position myself at the exit door, slowly open the door, and close it gently behind me. I observe the area in the atrium of the first floor where the conference room is positioned. There is no sign of Lynn or Dr. Mulcahy. I check my cell phone and there are no messages. I called Lynn's cell, and it rings, and then goes to her voicemail. I call Dr. Mulcahy, and she picks up the phone after the second ring. I immediately ask, "Bonnie, is Lynn, okay? What happened? Where is she?" There was a long pause, which seemed like an eternity, but really it was only about five seconds.

Dr. Mulcahy responds, "Josh, Lynn is with me in my office. Please join us here as soon as you can. I need to get back to the Board meeting for the other agenda items on today's schedule. I have already informed the Board that I will be a little bit late getting back and told them to continue with the other items, and I will catch up with them. We really have to talk but right now I don't have a lot of time."

I rush over to Bonnie's office, which is about eight minutes in brisk walking across our company campus. By the time I reach her office, I am out of breath and noticeably perspiring from the stress of the morning and the brisk walk. I take my jacket off and knock on the closed door. Dr. Mulcahy immediately invites me in and tells me to close the door behind me. Lynn is sitting with her arms positioned neatly on Dr. Mulcahy's conference table, and she is just staring at her folded hands. She has a look of solemnity and sadness in her eyes. I gently sit down at the seat next to her and put my hands softly over hers. Lynn looks at me and the tears start flowing down her cheeks. Dr. Mulcahy remains in silence.

The first words that come out of my mouth appear to be less than comforting. "Lynn, are you okay? What just happened in that conference room?" Lynn takes out a tissue and wipes her eyes while she gets her composure. "Josh, I couldn't answer the Board member's question." I look at Lynn and gently say to her, "Do you remember what the Board member asked you about?" Lynn looks at me as a little child would look at her father after being scolded. The look on her face was nothing less than pathetic. I could not help but feel so insensitive and uncaring at this time. I knew the answer to that question, but I asked the question anyway. It wasn't the answer that I wanted. The answer that I wanted was the whole reason that we had been planning to meet with the Board since August 2021 and start a new venture for our company. This was all evaporating right before my eyes.

At this point, Dr. Mulcahy excuses herself and tells us we can use her office for as long as we need to, until we get settled. She says her goodbyes and leaves to join her fellow Board members and continue the meeting where we left off.

After she leaves, Lynn and I are looking at each other. Finally, I say to Lynn, "Baby, do you want to go home? We can talk all about this when we get home. It can wait." Lynn looks up at me as the tears start streaming down her eyes, and she says, "Josh, hold on a minute. What I have to say can't wait. Two weeks ago, I was out jogging like we usually do. I roamed about six blocks from our house and then proceeded to come back. About halfway back to our house, I couldn't remember what street I needed to take to get back home. Everything was new to me and my surroundings, as if I have seen it for the first time."

I look at Lynn and say to her, "Lynn, why didn't you tell me? You must've been so scared and felt so alone." Lynn continued. "Josh, three days later, when you left for the office in your car and I said I would be late to the office because I had a meeting at Jessica's school, I was late for her meeting because I forgot where her school was. Finally, we got there, and I apologized to her teaching assistant for being late because, because … I told her I got a flat tire. Jessica knew something was wrong and just looked at me." That afternoon when you were out having lunch with one of our clients, I made an appointment to see a friend of Dr. Pereira's at Los Angeles Hospital, in the Department of Neurology." Lynn paused again as the tears really started coming down her cheeks.

"Josh, last week my test results came back. I have Early Onset Alzheimer's Disease."

Chapter 4
Lessons Learned

Lynn and Jessica perform meditation and reflection exercises before breakfast.

Josh recognizes that he wasted valuable years by neglecting to maintain a nurturing relationship with his family.

When making breakfast, Josh noticed something strange in the interaction between Lynn and Jessica. Lynn is unable to complete sentences in a game they are playing.

Josh questions whether he is overreacting to the situation, or whether it is a cause for concern. He is experiencing PTSD from the trauma Lynn went through last year in dealing with her medical condition.

Lynn drives herself and Josh to their meeting with Dr. Mulcahy and the Board of Directors.

Lynn gets lost on the route she has taken many times, to where she works on Medical Solutions Way.

Lynn arrives at the meeting flustered that she had missed the turn that she took for many years to get to work.

Josh reflects that the purpose of the meeting is to convince the Board to accept the vision statement for Differencia. The core values of the new company must be firmly established.

Dr. Mulcahy gavels the meeting to order at 10:00 AM. The first items on the agenda are the approval of the new vision statement and a ratification of a mission statement.

Differencia's vision statement is read to the Board.

Lynn is unable to explain to a Board member the difference between the vision statements for Medical Solutions and Differencia. Lynn sobs and abruptly leaves the meeting. Dr. Mulcahy leaves the meeting after Lynn's departure.

Upon reflection, Josh decides to exit the meeting, indicating that he will forward to the Board a mission and vision statement for Differencia.

Josh calls Dr. Mulcahy and asks her if Lynn is ok. Dr. Mulcahy tells him to meet her and Lynn in her office.

Lynn is in Dr. Mulcahy's office, and she is sobbing. She indicates that she was unable to answer the Board member's question.

Dr. Mulcahy leaves her office and returns to the Meeting Room to continue the meeting.

Lynn tells Josh that two weeks ago, she got lost while jogging and could not find her way home. Three days after this, Lynn forgot where Jessica's school was located.

Lynn is examined at the Department of Neurology at Los Angeles Hospital, and is told that she has Early Onset Alzheimer's Disease.

Questions to Ponder

Meditation is often recommended to reduce stress and improve the quality of decision-making. Do you practice daily meditation? If so, what meditation practices do you engage in? If not, are you willing to begin meditation? There are many meditation practices available on the Internet.

Do you focus on developing a nurturing relationship with your family each day? If so, how do you do this? If not, what can you do to strengthen the relationship you have with your family?

Is Josh's serious concern with Lynn's forgetfulness justified? Why or why not? Is he overreacting? What would you do differently? Are you currently experiencing a similar situation in your family?

Was Dr. Mulcahy's departure from the meeting appropriate? How would you have acted? Explain. Was Josh's exit from the meeting justified? Why or why not? Was it appropriate for him to promise to send the mission and vision statements later?

Although there is currently no cure for Alzheimer's disease, there are many steps one can take to slow its progression. Activities which stimulate mental activity can be beneficial. What activities do you engage in daily to stimulate your mind?

Social connectedness can slow down the progression of Alzheimer's and preserve executive function. What social connections do you have? Do you volunteer or engage in competitive mind games such as chess and bridge? How can you increase your social connectedness? Please identify two such activities.

Key Leadership Qualities Identified

Legitimate Concern - Clearly recognizing one's emotions and feelings from moment to moment. Not "catastrophizing" every event. Seeing the "big picture."

Mental Stimulation - Engaging in activities that exercise the mind and increase the use of our cerebral processes. Examples are gameshows such as Wheel of Fortune and Jeopardy. Also, playing the piano and learning a new language.

Social Connectedness - Interacting with others daily. Assisting others in their daily lives. Visiting with the elderly who are confined, and volunteering at a food pantry are good examples.

World View - We are all part of the universe and not just part of our immediate surroundings, such as our country or our neighborhood. Shakespeare sums it up best: "The world is a stage upon which each person must play his part."

Steadfastness - Accepting what happens to us and reacting constructively to it. Not giving in to adversity, even when it is severe. Alzheimer patients can engage in daily activities which will slow the progression of the disease.

Chapter 5

Authentic Loyalty and Authentic Leadership

The drive home from Dr. Mulcahy's office was quiet and somber. There were absolutely no words to describe what Lynn just shared with me. Our lives were shattered in that conference room, in a few seconds when Lynn could not remember the question asked by the Board member. It was simply to ascertain whether there was a difference between the old mission statement ratified by then, Medical Solutions, and the new one Lynn and I drafted for Differencia. It was so fundamental yet so complex for Lynn to answer. How could this be? Just last month, I asked Lynn to be my wife. I wanted her to be my life and my wife. Life is just so unfair. We hit one obstacle after another and always seem to survive. I do not know if we can survive this obstacle with Lynn's prognosis.

Lynn and I are supposed to be able to run this company on equal footage. This is much more than a business agreement. It represents similar leverage of shared thought and responsibility. How can an airplane survive in the air with only one wing? I know how to be an outstanding Director of Operations. I have held this job for several years and understand my craft, at least as well as anyone in my wheelhouse. I have never been a "Chief Executive Officer" of any company. I need Lynn to help me in this role. I need a mentor who understands me, knows how I operate, and can guide me where I need to go next to fulfill my duties as the top person in the company reporting to the Board of Directors.

We finally arrive at our townhouse. Jessica will not be home for a couple of hours. I will need to pick her up from school and make sure Lynn is okay. She still hasn't said a word. She sits at the kitchen table with her hands folded on her lap and her eyes fixated on the backsplash of the sink faucet. I slowly walk over to the kitchen table, sit next to Lynn, gently grab her hands from her lap, and place them on the table, putting my hands over hers. Her hands are cold and clammy. Her complexion is milky white, almost flushed. I say to Lynn softly and gently, "Lynn, are you okay?" Lynn nods affirmatively and asks me to get her a tall glass of water. Her palate and lips appear dry. She is fidgeting in her seat.

I get Lynn a glass of water and add ice cubes from the icemaker. Lynn takes a sip and thanks me. She looks at me and begins to crack a smile. "Josh, are you forgetting something?" I look at Lynn and softly say to her, "I don't think so, Lynn." She sharply responds, "Josh, who is running the company right now? Did you leave Dr. Mulcahy in charge? Although she is the Chairperson of the Board of Directors, you are still her boss as CEO of Differencia, and she is still the department head of the scientific laboratory. She may be at a Board meeting all day, but I do not think her responsibility is to run the company. That is your responsibility."

I respond sharply to Lynn, "I do not need to be reminded of my responsibility. Something happened to my life partner, soon to be my wife, and my place is with her right now." Lynn responds sharply, "You just don't get it, Josh, do you? It isn't about you and me. It is about everybody that you and I are responsible for. You didn't get it when I was sick with the possible aneurysm before. You still don't get it now when I have just been diagnosed with early-onset Alzheimer's."

I don't know how to respond to Lynn. She is right. I need to be aware of all my surroundings, personal and professional. Before I can say another word, Lynn grabs both my hands. "Dr. Mulcahy will be coming out of her meeting sometime this afternoon with a full plate. We are only one of her agenda items. I am only one of your agenda items right now, Josh. As much as you think the universe revolves around me, it doesn't. You are in control right now as my right-hand person, personally and professionally. We are now officially Co-CEOs."

I observe Lynn's facial expressions, as she is sitting on the edge of her chair. Why does she now have this chronic disease? Hasn't she been through enough? She has virtually saved the company from destruction by always being straightforward and truthful with her colleagues.

I look up to her and gently say, "We can still do this together, Lynn. We can get this new company off the ground and influence its success." Lynn softly replies, "Josh, you need to get back to work. I need to get myself settled and process what has been happening to me. I need to get continued medical advice to understand the extent of my incapacity. I need to know how long I have before I can no longer do my job. I need to know when I will have to resign from my current position. I need to feel confident that you can run this company without my assistance." My eyes begin to well-up. "This is not going to be easy, Josh. You must do this with me, and we can no longer fight about it."

Lynn was mentally and physically challenged. However, her instincts and posture remained strong and sound. I realized that we have a long road together going forward, personally and professionally. Life's roller coaster has undoubtedly taken us all for a loop. At every turn, this is a challenge. Nothing ever runs smoothly, the way you think you might want it to.

Finally, I feel the calm coming over me once again. I stand up in my chair at the kitchen table and tell Lynn I need to get back to work and see what is happening. Lynn smiles at me and tells me that we will talk later. On my way back to the office, I begin thinking about what just happened today and, more importantly, what led to it. Lynn hadn't mentioned the recent jogging event, when she forgot how to get home. She hadn't told me that she got lost going to Jessica's school the other day. I only noticed that something was wrong when I heard her doing her morning learning and reflection gymnastics with Jessica.

I never paid attention to the details of events surrounding my environment. I was too caught up in my world and agenda. This was not because of any superego on my part. It is just that I expected everything that mattered in life and business to come to me rather than the other way around. I realize now that I must deal with my environment and not blame others when I neglect to do so. This is what leadership is about. Isn't it?

Leaders need to realize that they are not victims of their fates. Instead, they are innovators of required changes and challenges. These changes and challenges require methodical planning from the leader and those that support the vision. This defines trust and loyalty. To be clear, this is not trust and commitment to one or more individuals on personal merit. To be authentic as a leader, you need to have trust and loyalty to principles and core values. This is all defined in Differencia's vision. This is what Lynn and I have been preparing for over the last eight months, when the last major scandal occurred at Medical Solutions. This was the training ground for what was to come next. After returning home from work tonight, I will talk with Lynn about a demanding and challenging day for Differencia and us. I need to be that authentic leader from now on. For my readers, I need your help and support to get me to that necessary plateau. Let us work this out together as my story evolves with this new challenge and a new beginning.

Chapter 5
Lessons Learned

Josh and Lynn drive home from Dr. Mulcahy's office.

Josh reflects upon Lynn's medical condition and prognosis and worries about his fortitude in dealing with it effectively.

Without Lynn at his side, Josh questions his ability to perform effectively as CEO.

Upon returning home, Josh asks Lynn how she is feeling.

Lynn admonishes Josh for not taking responsibility for running Differencia.

Josh defends himself by saying he has been focused on Lynn's medical condition. He laments her condition and credits her for saving Differencia from destruction.

Lynn tells Josh that she must concentrate on her incapacitation and that he must concentrate on leading Differencia without her assistance.

Josh recognizes the challenge he has been given and that he must be laser-focused on his efforts to lead Differencia.

Josh realizes that he must accept the current environment and not blame others for his current circumstance.

True leaders recognize that they are not victims of their fates but must be innovators and develop solutions to their challenges.

Josh muses that authentic leaders need to have trust and loyalty to principles, causes, and core values.

Josh asks readers for assistance in developing approaches to successfully lead Differencia.

Questions to Ponder

A recurring theme is that Josh exhibits a lack of confidence in dealing with adversity. Do you agree with this characterization of Josh? Why or why not? Do you have this character trait? If so, explain.

Is Josh too overwhelmed by Lynn's medical condition? Should he be more supportive of her by suggesting activities that she can engage in to improve her mental acuity? What activities would you recommend?

Is Lynn's criticism of Josh justified? Should she be more sympathetic to his plight? Have you ever been faced with a similar plight? If so, how did you react? In looking back, should you have reacted differently?

Authentic leaders accept their environment and realize that they must not feel victimized but must develop innovative solutions to their challenges. Do you agree with this? Why or why not? What innovative approaches have you developed to challenges you have encountered in the past?

Do you solicit assistance from others in addressing daily challenges? If so, explain how you do this. Have you found this approach leads to better decision-making?

Key Leadership Principles Identified

Acceptance - Being mindful of the current environment. This means understanding the forces at work in the moment. Stoicism is an excellent way of cultivating this.

Fortitude - The commitment to react to adversity with firm resolve. Never, never, never give up.

Support of Others - Helping others in addressing their daily challenges. This involves having empathy for those we associate with and offering constructive advice.

Patience - Recognizing that some challenges require long-run solutions. A good example is addressing the challenge of global warming. "Life is a marathon, not a sprint." Understanding the current environment and recognizing what one can control. In the words of St. Francis of Assisi, "God grant me the serenity to change the things I can, accept the things I can't, and the wisdom to know the difference."

Innovation - Implementing experimental approaches to discovering new knowledge. The discovery of electricity by Benjamin Franklin and the invention of the light bulb by Thomas Edison are clear examples.

Altruism - Concern for the welfare of others. Putting the interests of others above our own interests. It is based upon the belief that we are all part of a larger universe.

Chapter 6
Lynn, Josh, And Jessica

It is Sunday, April 24th at 9:00 AM. To say the least, so far it has been a stressful, yet very uneventful weekend. We spent most of Saturday after the Board meeting reflecting, gathering our thoughts, and trying to think through our next steps. Jessica has been very moody this morning and staying very much to herself. She knows that something is going on with her mom, but she has not said anything to either me or Lynn about it.

This is our usual time to go out and buy our Sunday breakfast and bring it back home. Lynn always waits for us to get back home, about twenty minutes from when we leave the house. We follow with breakfast together as a family, and discuss the highlights of the weekend and what we want to do for fun on our "Sunday Fun Day!"

This Sunday, things are a little different. I always wait for Jessica at the front door at 9:00 AM, but she has not yet come out of her room. She does not even have her coat on and is sitting with her arms folded and legs crossed in her bed. She is rocking back and forth. This is something I have never seen her do before. I call Lynn from across the room adjacent to our front door and she comes running. "What's wrong Josh?" I point my hand in the direction of Jessica's room and she looks at Jessica, rocking back and forth with her arms folded and legs crossed on her bed.

Lynn looks at me sternly. "Take off your jacket, Josh, and go to your daughter. She needs you now." I look at Lynn. "Lynn, she needs her mother, not her father." My response is simple. "Lynn, I cannot comfort her like you do. You are her mother." Lynn responds. "Josh, what are you going to do when I can't comfort her anymore? What are you going to do when you need to take care of me and Jessica? What are you going to do when you need to run Differencia? You must start thinking about this now, Josh! Sooner or later, this will be your reality."

I respond, "No Lynn, this is my hell! This is my punishment, to be subjected to pain and torture for watching the people I love and care about suffering around me. I don't deserve this. It is not fair." Lynn fires back to me, "Josh, I'll tell you what's not fair. What's not fair is going to St. Jude's Children's Hospital or Shriner's Hospital and watching innocent children dying of incurable cancers. What did they ever do to deserve their fates? Tell me Josh!" The tears begin streaming down Lynn's cheeks. "You are the dumbest, stupidest, most impulsive idiot on the planet right now." I am in shock and awe from what Lynn is saying to me.

"Lynn, how can you say these things to me and insult me like that?" Lynn responds, "Josh, I was listening to a radio show the other day while driving to work, and it had this leadership expert on the show. He was being interviewed about his perspective on what made him successful. His name was Dr. Cuomo, I think." I asked Lynn what he said that stuck in her mind. She retrieved her thoughts slowly on what Dr. Cuomo said. "I get up every time I fall. I never lose. I either win or learn." Josh, right now, this is the type of quote that you need to remember, dealing with your daughter. If you fall when trying to console her, learn what you are doing wrong and pretend I'm not there. You got to figure out what to do Josh! I don't know how much longer I will be lucid for the both of you."

"Lynn, we don't yet know the extent of your dementia. They are still going to run more tests and we must look at every possibility to keep you going at a normal pace." Lynn bounces back, "Josh, you need to be a realist and understand the gravity of what you are dealing with. More importantly, you also need to understand what needs to be done to keep our company going, and continue the legacy that we started together. You do not have the luxury of time to ponder on the past or the present. You must start thinking of the future."

I become much more pensive and feel the calm that I always feel, when I stabilize myself and get by the emotional fog that always holds me back. Speaking of quotes makes me think about something I read a long time ago. It was a quote by Winston Churchill: "If you're going through hell, keep going." If right now I am going through my hell, I must stop feeling sorry for myself and thinking about what could happen, and start thinking about what needs to happen if I am going to keep this company afloat.

I realize that my first obligation is to go into Jessica's room and find out why she isn't going with me to get breakfast for the three of us. We are already 15 minutes late for our usual 9:00 run and I want to know why.

I walk into Jessica's room very slowly and quietly. She has stopped rocking back and forth, but remains on the bed, staring at the wall across from her and humming to herself. I don't know what she is humming. I get close enough to listen to her. I can't believe what she is humming. I get the message right away. She is humming, "The itsy-bitsy spider went up the water spout. Down came the rain and washed the spider out. Out came the sun and dried up all the rain. And the itsy-bitsy spider went up the spout again."

I slowly grab Jessica's folded arms and open them up slowly. I grab her tiny hands and put my hands over her hands. She puts her head up slowly and our eyes meet. Her face suddenly reddens, and the tears started streaming from her eyes. Jessica says to me, "Daddy, mommy is sick, isn't she? You can tell me. I can figure it out. When I was in school and she told the school aide that she got a flat tire, I knew that was not the reason. She got lost, Daddy. She got lost!" I was left speechless and unaware how brilliant this little girl was, and how sensitive she was to everything going on around her.

Looking at Jessica, I see Lynn in her eyes. She is aware that she is facing the reality that she is no longer just losing her mother physically, but also losing her mentally. I grab a tissue and wipe the tears from the cheeks of her tiny face. I lament her suffering and the grief we both share. I realize how connected the three of us are. I know we all must get through this together.

The calm in me continues. "Jessica, let's try to make this a normal day, get breakfast, and bring it to Mommy. The three of us will talk and ask questions together. We may not have the answers to all the questions. What we will do is find out how we can all be together and get through this storm. When the sun comes back out, we will celebrate like we did before."

Jessica smiles at me. "Daddy, you are so silly. The sun doesn't have to come out for us to celebrate, if we are all together." I look at Jessica, "Are you sure you are only five years old?" Jessica smiles at me. "So are you, Daddy. So are you!" Jessica grabs my hand. "Let's get breakfast, Daddy!"

We bring breakfast to Lynn. All three of us have a great day together. We reminisce, laugh with one another, and enjoy each other's company. We all know that there will be scary days ahead. However, we are all confident that no matter what happens, we will get through it, together.

Tomorrow is going to be a big day, as Lynn and I are going to meet with Dr. Mulcahy at 9:00 AM sharp in her office. We will discuss how we are going to proceed going forward, with Lynn's most recent diagnosis.

Lessons Learned

On Sunday, April 24, Jessica is isolated in her room and is very moody. She senses that something is wrong with Lynn.

Jessica rocks back and forth on the bed with her arms and legs.

Lynn tells Josh to minister to their daughter.

When Josh responds that he cannot tend to Jessica's sadness, Lynn admonishes him for being self-centered and asks him what he will do when it comes time to take care of her and Jessica and run Differencia.

Josh laments that his current situation is punishment for his past neglect of Lynn and Jessica.

Lynn admonishes Josh for his self-pity and tells him that his current situation pales by comparison to children dying of incurable cancer.

Lynn tells Josh that he must be resilient and take charge of his current situation. He cannot play the role of the defenseless victim.

Josh needs to concentrate on the future and ignore the past and present. He needs to develop innovative approaches in dealing with the challenges he will be facing.

Adversity must be addressed by persevering and never giving up. "Failure is not an option."

Jessica is in her room humming the tune "Itsy-bitsy spider."

Jessica tells Josh that she realizes that her mother is sick.

Josh tells Jessica that she, Lynn, and Josh will work through Lynn's medical condition together.

Josh and Lynn plan to meet with Dr. Mulcahy the next morning to discuss how to deal with Lynn's Alzheimer's diagnosis.

Questions to Ponder

Is Jessica's reaction to Lynn's condition typical for a five-year-old? Why or why not?

Is Josh's feeling of helplessness in dealing with Lynn's condition justified? Why or why not? Have you ever been faced with such a situation?

Is Lynn reacting unreasonably in criticizing Josh for being self-absorbed? Explain your answer. What would you have done differently?

Josh constantly laments his situation and fails to change his ways and become more proactive. In the words of Winston Churchill "When you are in a hole, stop digging."

What can Josh do to become more connected to the world around him?

What innovative approaches can Josh develop to address his current situation? Fully explain your answer.

In your daily life, do you focus extensively on the past and present as opposed to the future? What can you do to become more future oriented?

How do you respond to adversity? Do you lament your plight? If so, how can you overcome this tendency?

Do you think that Jessica, at the age of five, can effectively deal with Lynn's illness with the absence of support?

How can Josh, Lynn, and Jessica effectively deal with Lynn's condition? What would you recommend they do?

Chapter 7
Josh, Lynn, And Dr. Mulcahy

It is Monday, April 26th, at 9:00 AM, and today we have a different agenda. We are meeting with Dr. Mulcahy to discuss what happened at the Board meeting last Friday. Board members were shocked, especially when Lynn could not answer a straightforward question directed to her. The question was rudimentary, in that a first-grade student could answer it, having the correct information to back it up. It was apparent to the Board that there was something serious going on with Lynn when she could not answer a question that she had been researching for the past eight months.

We arrive at Dr. Mulcahy's office at 9:00 sharp, and she was waiting for us. She has coffee, tea, muffins, and sweet rolls. She has blocked out three hours for us on her calendar, and is scheduled to meet with the Board in an emergency meeting this afternoon at 4:00 PM. A follow-up meeting will also be held. Lynn and I will address the Board as Co-CEOs of Differencia.

After reading through her notes and checking her calendar, Dr. Mulcahy brings us forward to open our meeting with a small prayer. "Dear Lord, please give us the guidance, wisdom, and understanding of meeting the challenges of what is to come with ourselves and our new company." Dr. Mulcahy pauses for some further reflection and continues her prayer. "Enable us to be precipitators of the truth. Please let us know what we can control and give equal latitude to what we can't control. Most importantly, please give us the wisdom and courage to know the difference. Amen."

Considering her being a brilliant scientist, Dr. Mulcahy shows herself to be a deep, spiritual thinker and believer that all good things will come if you believe you can accomplish them. It reminds me of a quote I saw many years ago working for Boston Biotech. I had to visit the Prudential Center to discuss the premiums on my insurance policy. The quote was on a plaque in a frame on the wall in the reception area. The quote read, "The best way to prepare for the future is to create it." It makes a lot of sense to me now. The best way to create history is to use the resources that we presently have available to us and make the most of them. However, the most important thing is to know where those resources live, internal and external to our organization.

Somehow all this fits into our new vision for Differencia. The hard part is putting the mission and strategic plan into the vision. All of this is a bunch of words unless we put it into practice. We also must realize that the new company will create a new culture. We will do a lot of the same things. However, we will do them differently. We will be more diverse in approach to solving problems.

Medicine is unique in many ways and provides opportunities for individuals to heal from certain illnesses. However, not everyone responds to these medicines in the same way. Many of them are very effective in treating certain diseases. However, others have consequential side effects that may do more harm than good to the individuals taking these drugs.

At this point, scientific research is necessary to give many deserving individuals the opportunity to live a healthier, stable, and resourceful life, despite their age and ability to pay for these drugs.

My thoughts are continuing to consume me to the point where it appears I am phasing out from the members of this meeting. Suddenly, Dr. Mulcahy says to me, "Josh, are you here with us right now?" She cries out and smiles, "Mentally, that is." We all begin laughing, which serves as an excellent icebreaker to our very serious conversation, which is yet to come this morning.

Dr. Mulcahy begins the meeting by looking at Lynn and saying to her, "Lynn, if at any time you feel pressured or uncomfortable answering any of my questions, I want you to let me know as soon as possible. I intend to put us all in the right perspective, considering what transpired at our Board meeting. I also want you to realize that everyone on the Board, including myself, knows that what happened was beyond your control."

Lynn becomes very pensive and folds her hands on Dr. Mulcahy's meeting table. She stares at them and then looks up at Dr. Mulcahy and says, "Bonnie, three weeks ago, I was out jogging in a six-block radius around my house. I had run about a mile and a half in total. Three-quarters of the way back to my house, I realized I could not remember how to get back home. I panicked, sat down on the curbstone on East Street, and had to think hard about retracing my steps of how I got to the point where I was presently sitting. It took me 20 minutes to figure it out."

Dr. Mulcahy looks at Lynn most pensively and asks her to continue after a brief pause. "Bonnie, I knew something was wrong with me, and I felt emotions that were so overwhelming. I thought I would pass out from the fear of what just happened."

I hand a glass of water over to Lynn and ask her if she is okay. She acknowledged me and continued her story, staring at her folded hands. "I finally made it back to my house and didn't tell anyone what had happened. I thought this might've been a flashback, due to PTSD, when I took a seizure on a plane traveling from Boston to LAX eight months ago and never made it back home. You all know the story from there. I went about my merry way, and everything seemed normal at work, at home, and playing word games with my daughter Jessica early morning before work. We always spend quality time together. It is the highlight of my day, especially in the morning."

Lynn paused and the tears just fell freely from her cheeks as her eyes welled up. She took a handkerchief from her purse, took a deep breath, and continued talking with her voice cracking and unsteady in pitch and tone. I started singing our favorite song together, one of which I sang to Jessica from the first time I held her in my arms and I. …and I…and I, completely forgot the words to one of the song's lines.

"The following week, I met Jessica at her school with her teaching aide. The meeting was supposed to be held at 9:00 sharp. Driving her to school, which I have done a thousand times, I couldn't remember the street where I needed to turn to get to her school building. I was horrified. Eventually, I remembered the street that would get us there. I was only about 10 or 12 minutes late. I told the aide I had a flat tire and apologized for being late. I lied Bonnie, in front of my daughter. I could have died because Jessica knew what happened when she was in the car with me." Lynn continued. "I didn't tell anyone about this incident as well. I even kept it from Josh. Forgive me, Josh."

I nod at Lynn affirmatively and put my hand over her hand to give her comfort and support. Lynn continues, "That Tuesday afternoon, I contacted Dr. Pereira, the neurologist who treated me at Los Angeles County Medical Center. He was the doctor responsible for saving my life and figured out that the files on me were mixed up with another patient. I trust him implicitly. He arranged for me to have some tests and then see a neuropsychologist right away. Wednesday afternoon, the next day, I saw the neuropsychologist recommended by Dr. Pereira, who was one of the best in diagnosing and treating dementia and Alzheimer's disease."

Dr. Mulcahy asked me at this point if I wanted a break. I looked at Lynn, and she nodded no; she wanted to continue. "The neuropsychologist's name is Dr. Louis Friedman, a Harvard Senior Fellow and one of the top neuropsychologists in the country. He asked me questions for over two and a half hours. He gave me a battery of tests that exhausted me, inside and out. Most importantly, he was interested in my executive functioning. At the end of the testing, he told me that things appeared to be normal for the time being and recommended a series of CAT scans and blood tests. He told me that he would have the results in about two weeks."

Lynn continued. "On April 16th, my test results came back. The prognosis was not good. I was diagnosed with Early-Onset Alzheimer's disease. I got on the phone immediately with Dr. Friedman and asked for clarification. I asked to what extent would the disease consume me, to the point I would become incapacitated and no longer be capable of working at my job? I will not bore you with all the medical details and the intricacies of our very long meeting that afternoon, in his office after our phone call. He put a considerable amount of time aside to speak with me with medical professionalism, and an enormous amount of uncertainty about the progression of my disease. He recommended more tests and set up another appointment for me. The new appointment is May 23rd at 1:00 PM, to get a progress report."

Dr. Mulcahy looked at me with tenderness, apprehension, fear, and empathy all at the same time. I nod at Lynn, indicating that she should say something at this point. Dr. Mulcahy slowly turns toward Lynn and gently says, "Lynn, have you been prescribed any medication between now and when you have your next appointment with Dr.

Friedman?" Lynn responds, "Bonnie, I am not on any medication right now." Dr. Mulcahy clarifies to Lynn that she does not have to say anything to the Board about this at her meeting today. She is protected by HIPAA laws and is under no obligation to give any of this information without her permission.

I believe that I must chime in and say something. "Lynn is entitled to her privacy. She doesn't have to disclose any of this to the Board until we have more follow-up tests, as to the extent of her dementia and how long it might be before it affects her ability to do her job." Dr. Mulcahy remained silent and looked over to Lynn for a response. It was clearly a look of empathy rather than solace. Dr. Mulcahy could only envision the decisions Lynn will have to make, sooner than later. Lynn is lucid and on point with her choices most of the time.

I chime in again. "What if it is a misdiagnosis? We just had a situation less than a year ago where doctors were going to put a drill through Lynn's head to relieve pressure on her brain. It was Dr. Pereira that prevented this from happening. We need to have more tests to confirm her diagnosis of Alzheimer's or dementia, whatever you want to call it."

Lynn pauses for a moment. Then, she puts her head in her hands and slowly straightens up. Her eyes are filled with moisture as she struggles to get the first words out of her mouth. Her head immediately turns in my direction. "Josh, don't you get it? I forgot how to get to Jessica's school. I was jogging close to our house, and I forgot how to get home. Last Friday, before our Board meeting, I forgot the words to a simple music jingle that I have been singing with Jessica since she was a baby. What more proof do you need, Josh, that this will not go away? Face the facts, please!"

At this point, I don't know what to say to Lynn. Further, I can't deny her words are probably accurate. However, I am not 100% convinced that her diagnosis leading up to this point is correct.

Dr. Mulcahy looks at her watch and says, "Lynn and Josh, I only have until noon today before I need to take care of some things at my job, and then go to a Board meeting explaining what happened last Friday. I can't go into that Board meeting with uncertainty and ambiguity. I need to be straight with the Board, or we will lose our transparency and trust with them. We need to think of the 11,000 people that we represent."

I look at Dr. Mulcahy with much less admiration now. What she just said makes me feel uncomfortable toward my wife. She immediately reads my facial expression and responds emphatically, "Josh, do you think I like what I just said? Remember, we are all in this together. We can't be in this two-thirds together. Any one of the three of us missing on this team to get this new company off the ground is catastrophic, and Differencia will fail." I look at her and strike back immediately, filled with anger. "Bonnie, if you take Lynn out of the equation now, I guess you should take me out too. That leaves you without a CEO!"

Lynn looks at me with horror and contempt. Dr. Mulcahy asked if we would like a few minutes to compose ourselves and return. Lynn says to her, "Bonnie, we will settle this right here and now if we are to have total transparency. We need to share one thing we all have in common, our dignity and trust for one another." Lynn suddenly looks at me and says to me, as the tears well up in her eyes and drop down her cheeks, "Josh, I love you. I truly do love you. However, before you existed in my life, I was doing the work that I loved and was in this company. Please do not make me choose which battle I must win to have you both. I don't think I can take that right now."

Dr. Mulcahy remained silent as Lynn continued. Lynn's face was reddened and flushed, and she came on to me as the adrenaline flowed through her body. "How dare you threaten to take away leadership at the helm of this company when it needs it the most. How dare you use me as a sacrificial lamb and declare yourself a hero by threatening the Chair of the Board of Directors. You are only trying to satisfy your ego by putting everyone in this company at risk to get your way. You have been like this your whole life."

Dr. Mulcahy remained silent, then insisted we take a ten minute break, or, as she put it, "a timeout." Lynn and I immediately left the meeting and stepped out into the atrium outside the office. We sit on opposite sides of each other, around an ornamental tree planted for decorative purposes. We remain silent. You could've cut the atmosphere around our heads with a knife. I check my smartwatch and the ten minutes are up. We walk back into the meeting with Dr. Mulcahy.

Dr. Mulcahy picks up the conversation just before we had the break. "Lynn and Josh, this will be difficult for all three of us. We must stop playing the blame game and own up to the facts. Josh, do you think you are ready to take over if Lynn becomes incapacitated or unable to do her job?" I look over to Lynn. Still, she will not look me in the eye. I respond to Dr. Mulcahy, "I'm not sure. There is a sharp learning curve, and I need a good mentor to help me lead as the company's top executive." Dr. Mulcahy responds, "Is that why you lashed out at Lynn the way you did? Because you were insecure on taking over the helm without Lynn's assistance?"

My reaction to Dr. Mulcahy is less emotional and I feel the calm once again. I respond to her question. "I guess that probably is true. I don't have enough confidence in myself to think I can do the job when Lynn becomes incapacitated." Dr. Mulcahy bounces back with a response. "Well, I'm glad we're being honest right now, Josh. I guess this is what transparency is truly all about. Lynn and I are both sympathetic to your learning curve, as we all had to learn our jobs once we were designated to be the best one to perform at it. For some of us, it was sooner than later."

Dr. Mulcahy continues. "I am prepared to tell the Board this afternoon that Dr. Lynn Ann Marconi had taken ill and that is the reason she abruptly left the meeting. The illness is currently under review by her doctors and poses no threat to her capacity to do her job at Differencia in the immediate future. If the situation changes, the Board will be notified immediately. Her partner, Josh Keating, will temporarily take over as CEO until Dr. Marconi's health situation is resolved."

Dr. Mulcahy asks both of us if we are comfortable with her statement to the Board. Lynn and I finally connect with mutual agreement and nod affirmatively toward her. She went on to say that the Board members might have an issue that Lynn could not answer a Board member's question that was so simple. It could raise some eyebrows on her statement to the Board on Lynn's condition. However, it could also be possible that Lynn received some very bad news about her health just before the meeting and could not focus on the Board member's question at the time. This could be an alibi for the time being. The meeting is adjourned, and Lynn and I leave the meeting holding hands, looking at each other, smiling, and shaking our heads.

On the way back to our offices, Lynn receives a call, and her smile quickly disappears from her face. I look at Lynn and ask her if everything is okay. She immediately puts her hand up to signal me to stop talking so she can hear what's going on at the other end of the phone. I immediately think something happened to Jessica at school. I start shouting, "Lynn, tell me, is this about Jessica? Is she okay?" Lynn puts her hand up again and tells me, "Josh, wait. I'll explain in a minute!" She apologizes to whoever is on the other end of the phone, and the conversation ends with a very abrupt "goodbye."

Lynn looks at me and says, "Dr. Friedman and Dr. Pereira want to see me at the LA Medical Center as soon as possible. They found something in my blood tests and need to explain it to me as soon as I can make an appointment. They said to tell the person making the appointment to get me in ASAP on this schedule, except for any emergencies."

My response to Lynn is to make the appointment and I will go with her. She puts her hand up to me once again in a very militant, stern manner. "Josh, again, do I have to remind you, you have a company to run. You need to get back to work and take care of anything that we would have to handle on the agenda for today. Take me out of the picture right now. You may have to do this sooner than later. I don't know what's coming. This may be your moment to shine. Have courage and do the right thing. I have confidence in you."

I look at Lynn as moisture builds in her eyes. She put her arms around me, hugs me tightly, and says, "Josh, I'm scared. I am only telling you this. It's not about me. It's about Jessica. She is our future, Josh. You must see this through. You'll know what to do. I have faith."

The calm returns. Lynn leaves me. She makes her appointment with the doctors at Los Angeles Medical Center. I return to work. I remember the words of John Paul Jones, "Damn the torpedoes. Full steam ahead!"

Chapter 7
Lessons Learned

Josh, Lynn, and Dr. Mulcahy plan to meet with the Board of Directors on Monday April 26.

Based upon her inability to answer a Board member's question last Friday, the Board senses that something is wrong with Lynn.

Dr. Mulcahy opens the Board meeting with a prayer asking for guidance as to how to proceed.

Josh reflects that the best way to assure the development of a meaningful mission and vision statement for Differencia is to formulate a plan.

Scientific research is necessary to provide deserving individuals with the opportunity to live a healthy and resourceful life, despite their age and ability to pay.

Dr. Mulcahy tells Lynn to remain calm and not worry about leaving the Board meeting abruptly.

Lynn responds by recounting episodes of forgetfulness over the past few weeks.

Lynn recounts a meeting with a teacher's aide at Jessica's school and getting lost and lying that she was late not because of a flat tire, but that she got lost.

Lynn tells Dr. Mulcahy that later that day, she met with Dr. Pereira and a neuropsychologist at Los Angeles Medical Center, and had a series of tests performed.

The test results indicated that Lynn has Early-Onset Alzheimer's disease.

Dr. Mulcahy tells Lynn that she does not have any obligation to inform the Board about the details of her current condition.

Josh muses that perhaps there is a misdiagnosis.

Lynn admonishes Josh for being a misbeliever and that he should be more connected with reality.

Dr. Mulcahy tells Josh and Lynn that she must be transparent with the Board and must express uncertainty as to Lynn's future with Differencia.

Josh threatens to resign from his role as Co-CEO if Lynn does not continue in her position.

Lynn reprimands Josh for his threat to resign and chastises him for being self-absorbed.

Dr. Mulcahy asks Josh if he feels capable of running Differencia if Lynn is absent.

Josh responds that he is not sure.

Lynn, Josh, and Dr. Mulcahy agree to tell the Board that Lynn's condition currently does not affect her ability to perform her Co-CEO duties at Differencia, and that if her situation changes, Josh will take over as CEO.

Dr. Pereira and Dr. Friedman ask to see Lynn at Los Angeles Medical Center to review the blood test results.

Lynn makes her appointment with the doctors at Los Angeles Medical Center and Josh returns to work.

Questions to Ponder

Dr. Mulcahy appears to have religious beliefs. Do you agree with her decision to open the Board meeting with a prayer? What would you have done differently?

Do you agree that the purpose of medical research is to provide individuals with the opportunity to have a healthy and resourceful life, despite their age and ability to pay?

Do you agree with Dr. Mulcahy's approach to managing the meeting?

Would you be concerned with Lynn's pattern of forgetfulness, or would you want further evidence to develop? Explain your answer. Have you ever encountered a similar situation? If so, how did you handle it?

Do you agree with Dr. Mulcahy's decision to not prod Lynn to divulge her medical condition to the Board?

Is Josh realistic in his view that the assessment of Lynn's condition could be a misdiagnosis? Explain your answer? Would you have reacted in a similar way?

Is Lynn's admonishment of Josh for not being connected to reality justified?

Is Dr. Mulcahy's decision to be transparent with the Board and to inform them of the uncertainty about Lynn's ability to continue in her current role a wise one? Explain your answer. Have you ever faced a similar circumstance?

Is Josh's assertion that he will resign from his role if Lynn is not retained, justified? Why do you think he reacted in this way? Is it insecurity? Is it anger?

Do you agree with Dr. Mulcahy's decision to retain Lynn in her current role until her condition changes? If not, what would you have done differently?

Key Leadership Qualities Identified

Religious Beliefs - Foundational principles based upon the tenet that belief in a higher power can improve one's decision-making.

Clarity of Purpose - Knowing what end goal should be achieved. Being focused on the desired income and not being diverted by distractions.

Socratic Method - Asking frequent questions to understand the goals and objectives of others. This is an excellent way of developing empathy for others.

Hippocratic Oath - As a physician, respecting the privacy of others regarding their medical condition. This leads to the development of trust, which is essential for authentic leadership.

Mindfulness - Being engrossed in the present moment. This is critical in developing insightful approaches to addressing the present challenge.

Equanimity - Evenness of mind, especially under stress. This leads to mental calmness, which leads to clarity of thought in decision-making.

Chapter 8
The Prognosis and Catharsis

Let it be known to our readers and followers who are used to hearing Josh's inner voices and thinking processes; we are taking a different approach in this chapter. We are writing to you about our experiences personally and professionally, chapter by chapter in our books. This chapter has a surprise for you. You are going to be reading about me, Dr. Lynn Ann Marconi. In this chapter, you will be listening to my inner thoughts and voices and not Josh's. Let the chapter begin!

Josh has returned to work, and I am on my way to see Dr. Friedman and Dr. Pereira this afternoon, Wednesday, April 27th, 2022, at 1:00 PM, to discuss my condition. Initially, my next appointment would not have been until mid-May. Something must've come up, making me very nervous about their sense of urgency. The way our lives have been going, we have not been able to find a sense of calm for almost a year, since I had my seizure in August 2021, which almost cost me my life.

My mind is going in so many different directions right now. I am only 43 years old, but feel like I've lived 100 years. Sometimes I could tear Josh apart, and other times, I feel like he is my rock, hope, and salvation. He is an enigma to me. It is almost as if Josh was my alter ego. We clash on many things. However, we wholeheartedly agree on our love for each other and our daughter Jessica.

My life is filled with challenges, joys, regrets, and triumphs. I have only lived half of that life, and I don't know how much longer I will be able to live the other half of it. This is what scares me the most. I do care what happens to me. Yet, at the same time, I am responsible for asking Josh to be my equal partner in running Differencia. He will oversee more than eleven thousand employees. This company is growing exponentially, based on its future aspirations of developing new life-saving drugs. I am not sure if Josh can handle all of this alone, without me helping him out. He needs to prove to the Board and to me that he can do the job in my absence.

I don't know how much longer I can work at my job in my present capacity and prognosis. We need to prepare both personally and professionally. This is going to be the greatest challenge of all. We need to stick together as a family. We need to be together through thick and thin, and carry ourselves through the waves until we reach a haven.

I am getting close to the Los Angeles Medical Center, and going to the West Wing of the hospital, where personal office visits are made in the department of neurology. It is 12:45 PM, and my appointment is at 1:00. I think I'll go to the vending machine and get myself a Diet Coke. For some reason or another, Diet Coke calms my nerves and makes me relax. Josh asked me to explain this. I can't. All I know is that it works. I get my Coke and check in with the front desk, and the attending medical clerk tells me they will notify Dr. Pereira and Dr. Friedman that I've arrived. I take my seat in the reception area outside of Dr. Pereira's office and patiently wait for the attendant to tell me I can go in to talk to the doctors.

My hands are clammy, and I can feel my face getting hot. I'm sure this is just a nervous reaction due to the stress leading up to this meeting with these doctors. Finally, the attendant is buzzed at the front desk, and I am escorted into Dr. Pereira's office. It is a massive office with two large, pillared lamps and a sizable mahogany desk. In front of the desk are two very comfortable leather seats. A vast brown circular leather couch surrounds a large glass coffee table on the far side of his office.

Dr. Friedman is seated in one of the leather seats in front of Dr. Pereira's large mahogany desk. He cordially takes my shawl and puts it on a coat hanger, in a closet behind his desk. He walks me over to the other leather seat and asks me to sit down and make myself comfortable. I am anything but comfortable, and I am tense. I am trying to relax, but feel the adrenaline flowing through my body as if I just had ten cups of coffee with espresso shots. Dr. Pereira asks me if I would like some water or anything else before starting our meeting. I nod no as I look up at the doctor, smiling nervously.

Dr. Pereira reiterates that if I want anything, to just let him know. I don't know what got into me, but I yell out to him in a semi-loud and forceful tone, "I have been through so much. I am so scared right now. Please tell me why you and Dr. Friedman asked me in here today. Please, you don't have to be polite anymore. Just give it to me straight, doctor to patient." I feel the tears streaming down my eyes uncontrollably, and I can't make them stop. Dr. Pereira gets up from behind his desk, and Dr. Friedman lifts himself from his seat, gesturing to Dr. Pereira to sit next to me and face me. Dr. Friedman gets some tissues and hands them to me to wipe my eyes dry, while explaining what is going on with his assistance. I immediately feel the calm as my heart slows down and my hands begin to warm up. Now I know what Josh meant when he said he felt the calm.

Dr. Pereira begins the conversation. "Lynn, I decided to use my instincts once again, about your blood test results, basically in the same manner as I did back in August 2021 after you responded, calling for your daughter when supposedly you'd suffered a severe aneurysm on your plane flight from LAX to Boston." I asked Dr. Pereira if there was something wrong with my blood tests. The doctor responded, "Lynn, this is the problem. Your blood tests came back without any abnormalities, with one exception. You have a much higher level than normal of a hormone called Cortisol. I found this quite interesting, and I consulted with Dr. Friedman."

Dr. Friedman continued where Dr. Pereira left off. "Dr. Pereira and I took another look at your Cortisol levels, and they were quite high. In the past year, based on my study of your situation, you have been experiencing continuing high levels of stress, both personally and professionally."

Dr. Friedman is the neuropsychologist who ran the battery of tests on me and studied my executive functioning intensely from all different angles, and found nothing remarkable in his findings. Dr. Pereira further explained that Dr. Friedman wants me to take another path and test my blood again for Cortisol levels, if my stress levels are reduced substantially over six months. When it is at higher-than-normal levels, it has been known to cause memory lapses.

At this point, I was getting frustrated with the conversation, and I yelled out to both doctors, "Well, do I have Alzheimer's or not? Am I suffering from onset dementia? Can I still act as CEO of my company? You are the medical people who tell me what I need to do." Dr. Friedman looked at me intensely and said in a very calm manner, "I want to monitor you over the next 3 to 6 months. If my suspicions are correct, you may not have early-onset Alzheimer's. You may be suffering from an increased amount of stress that is causing you to have memory lapses. These memory lapses may be related to your non-epileptic seizures. By your own admission, when you are in distress, exceptionally high levels of stress can cause you to have the seizure-like episodes."

Dr. Friedman continued. "Lynn, to understand the full extent of your illness and your capabilities of running the company, while adhering to your domestic responsibilities as a mother and life partner to Josh, you will need to take some time off from Differencia."

I look at Dr. Friedman as if he has three heads. I am still baffled, and ask for further clarification. "Are you saying I can go to work every day and run the company, with Josh as an equal partner?" Dr. Friedman replied, in no uncertain terms, that his professional recommendation to Dr. Mulcahy, as Chair of the Board of Directors at Differencia, would be to have me take six months off, away from my job, with the stipulation that a clean bill of health after six months of observation would enable him to decide on my health condition. Dr. Friedman stated that this is not something that he recommends on a whim. He tells me that he realizes that an entire company depends on my leadership, and his professional opinion has a consequence on that leadership.

Dr. Pereira then sits behind his desk, and Dr. Friedman takes his seat once again next to me. Dr. Pereira says, "Lynn, this is not a punishment, but could be salvation to your dilemma. We are medical people, and in our wheelhouses, are pretty good at our craft. We make professional judgments based on what we know and are trained to do. We are not always perfect, but we can save thousands of lives, day in and day out. Your life could have been lost if I didn't use my instincts, expertise, and experience, to know something was wrong with your prognosis."

I am now looking at Dr. Pereira with tears in my eyes. "Dr., you saved my life. You prevented a drill from going into my head, which could have killed me and would've been a mistake. I can never pay you back for what you did. I am realizing now, for the first time, that my running Differencia is far less important than what you did for me today. You and Dr. Friedman may have saved the welfare of thousands of employees and hundreds and thousands of patients by making this diagnosis of me today. As a CEO, my lapse in judgment could be crucial on the details of what I direct my employees to do and say about the drugs that we manufacture and distribute."

Dr. Pereira looks at me and hands me a large envelope containing his and Dr. Friedman's recommendations about me taking six months away from my job. These doctors tell me that they will trust me to give the suggestions to Dr. Mulcahy, and not put them in the mail or give them to anyone else to deliver to her.

Dr. Pereira looks at me and says, "Lynn, will there be anything else you need or want to say to me?" I look at him. "I don't think so." He chuckles and smiles, shake his head and responds this way: "Isn't there somebody else running this company with you?" I stutter, put my hand over my mouth, and gasp. "Yes, Dr., my future husband, Josh Keating." Dr. Pereira and Dr. Friedman clarified that I could be free to mentor and assist Josh while I am being evaluated. I take a sigh of relief, and they make me promise that when I feel stressed, to back off and let Josh do his job.

I look at Dr. Pereira and say, "How did you know Josh needed mentoring?" He smiles at me and says, "I am a pretty quick study, and it didn't take me long to know how much he depended on you, when he thought you were out of commission at this hospital, when you were taken in by ambulance with an alleged aneurysm!"

I smile at Dr. Pereira and shake hands with both doctors as I leave the medical center. I am relieved and puzzled at the same time about how I will address Josh and Dr. Mulcahy about my condition, and in the future as CEO of Differencia. I am on my way back to our condo and thinking of everything the doctors told me. However, what I am thinking about most is what role I will play in our family's future. I am also thinking about what role I will play going forward at Differencia. How will Josh be able to survive without me there for the next six months? How will Jessica like having me around, my genius child? Will I still forget my lines when we play "Finish the Phrases?"

For the first time in my professional career, I now realize that Josh, not me, will be at the helm of our new organization, Differencia. What type of leader will he be? Will he panic the same way he did when he thought I was missing last August? Will he panic again, like he did when he thought I had an aneurysm and might not recover? Listen to me speak to my thoughts. I am falling into the same trap that Josh fell into less than a year ago. I criticized him for it. Here I am doing the same thing. I am panicking. I am no longer playing the role of Josh's alter ego, but rather playing the role of his previous ego when I was in charge, and not realizing the difference.

I remember reading somewhere in an economics journal that economist Dr. Robert Cuomo wrote, "It is amazing what can be accomplished when you don't care who gets the credit."

Differencia is our company, no matter who is on the inside and who is on the outside. Another quote flashes in my head, but I can't remember where I heard it. It's funny sometimes how the brain works. Things come into your head related to your thoughts, and somehow, your brain sequences the commonalities of those thoughts to a problem you are trying to solve. The human mind is truly a fantastic thing. We often don't give it enough credit for what it does in the background, without us even thinking about it. Well, here is the quote that just came into my head: "Don't ever take a fence down until you know why it was put up." I remember it now; this quote came from one of the poetry classes I took as an elective in grad school, studying for my master's in finance. It came from the poet, Robert Frost!

This will be difficult for the three of us to absorb and process. The first thing I will do now is pick up my cell phone and call Josh. It's now 2:35 PM. Jessica gets out of school at 3:00. I'm on my way to pick her up, and yes, I remember how to get there. I will be on time, with bells on!

Oh yes, one more thing I want to share with my readers. In this book, in the future, my thoughts and Josh's thoughts will be on equal footage, so you will know what we are thinking and processing as we interact with the other characters in the storyline! Enjoy the journey with us as Differencia continues to evolve, along with Josh and me, into the future to find our roles in authentic leadership and continue to search for authentic leaders.

This journey will not be easy, but will be necessary. Leadership is always under construction. It is not an end to a means. It is the ship's bow, trying to find the horizon ahead. The ship is always pointed to the horizon, but it never entirely meets up with it. Leaders need to constantly be in search of fulfilling their own needs before they can fulfill the needs of others. Authentic leaders always have a yearning to make themselves better, but not perfect. They always desire to bring out the best in others and make them the best version of themselves. Now, let's move on to the Lessons Learned in this chapter of our lives.

Chapter 8

Lessons Learned

In this chapter, Dr. Lynn Marconi indicates that she will report her inner thoughts and emotions to the reader.

Lynn is on her way to see Dr. Pereira and Dr. Friedman to discuss her condition.

She reflects that Josh is her alter ego and that they share a love for each other and for Jessica.

Lynn worries about Josh's ability to run Differencia in her absence. She is unsure as to how much longer she can work in her current capacity and prognosis.

Lynn arrives at Dr. Pereira's office to meet with him and Dr. Friedman. She asks why she was called in for a meeting.

Dr. Pereira tells Lynn that her blood tests came back normal, without any abnormalities except for an elevated level of Cortisol.

Cortisol at elevated levels has been known to cause memory lapses.

Based on this information, Lynn wants to know if she should continue in her current role at Differencia.

Dr. Pereira tells Lynn that she may not have Early-Onset Alzheimer's, but that her forgetfulness could be caused by her high stress levels.

Dr. Pereira recommends that Lynn take some time off from Differencia. He says that after six months, he will be in a better position to decide if Lynn should resume her duties as Co-CEO.

Lynn thanks Dr. Pereira and Dr. Friedman for their assessment and that their approach to her condition will be in the best interests of fulfilling Differencia's mission and vision statements.

Dr. Pereira and Dr. Friedman tell Lynn that she is free to mentor Josh over the next six months.

After the meeting with Dr. Pereira and Dr. Friedman, Lynn thinks about how she will inform Josh and Dr. Mulcahy about her condition, and what role she will play in her family's future.

How will Josh survive in Lynn's absence and how will Jessica take to her being around?

Lynn reflects on her plight and recognizes that the next six months will give her the opportunity to decide on how to proceed.

Lynn wonders about what kind of leader Josh will be. Will he be strong, or will he be indecisive?

Future chapters will focus upon the reflections of both her and Josh.

Leadership is a process in which the leader fulfills his own needs before fulfilling the needs of others. This will lead to helping others "to become the best version of themselves."

Questions to Ponder

Jessica sees Josh as her alter ego. Do you have an alter ego? If so, who is it? What common goals do you share?

Are Lynn's doubts about Josh's ability to lead Differencia justified? Why or why not? Explain your answer. Have you experienced this feeling in your relationships?

Is Lynn's reaction to Dr. Pereira's and Dr. Friedman's report on Cortisol being a explanation for her condition reasonable? How would you have reacted? Have you ever experienced a similar situation in your past?

Do you agree with Dr. Pereira's and Dr. Friedman's recommendation that Lynn take a leave of absence from Differencia, before deciding if she should continue in her current role? Explain your answer. Would you recommend a different course of action?

In the final analysis, do you agree with Lynn's approval of Dr. Pereira's and Dr. Friedman's proposal. That it is in the best interests of Differencia?

How should Lynn inform Josh and Jessica about Dr. Pereira's and Dr. Friedman's proposal? What rationale should she use?

How should she package her message to Josh? How should she package the message to Jessica?

What activities should Lynn engage in over the next six months to best decide how to proceed?

Key Leadership Qualities Identified

Alter Ego - A person or entity vicariously liable for another. Being concerned with the welfare of others. The belief that we are all born with altruistic tendencies.

Commonality of Purpose - Having the same goals and objectives of others. This leads to the development of leadership influence. This involves strategically interacting with others to understand their mindset.

Positive Message Delivery - Conveying messages in a constructive light. Explaining to others how a challenge can be effectively addressed. In the words of Eleanor Roosevelt, "I would rather light a candle than curse the darkness."

Understanding the Current Environment - Being aware of the situational landscape. What forces are at play in the environment which will affect the effectiveness of a decision? Explain.

Goal Delegation - Explaining to others one's goals and objectives, and allowing them to address the challenges in their own way. This involves trusting their ability to achieve their goals and objectives effectively.

Anticipation - Sensing what comes next. In the words of the basketball great Bill Russell, "I had the rebound before he took the shot."

Chapter 9
Dinner April 27th, 2022

I am home now with Jessica and waiting for Josh to return home, so I can explain everything to my family about my meeting with Doctors Pereira and Freidman. On Friday, April 28th, I will be meeting with Josh and Dr. Mulcahy to discuss alternate plans for Differencia, considering the new information given to me today by my physicians.

It is 4:00. Jessica asks me if I want to order out before her father gets home. I respond, "Jess, how would you feel if we made dinner together for Daddy?" Jessica seems uncomfortable with the suggestion and retreats to her room and closes her door. I don't know what to make of her abrupt behavior to this suggestion. All I asked her was if she would like to make dinner with me and surprise her father tonight, instead of ordering out.

I think I'll give Jessica a few minutes as a timeout before I go into her room and ask her what is wrong. I really want to know why she reacted the way she did over a very simple question. This is so unusual. I thought she would jump at the chance to make dinner with me. We would bond together, and we would maybe even sing a song together. This could be so much fun! Why is she resisting me like this?

I am realizing for the first time that true parenting is a lot more stressful than I thought, perhaps even more stressful than running a company like Differencia. I can imagine how Josh must've felt when he learned I was missing and maybe even losing me to a brain aneurysm. I guess I am getting a taste of my own medicine and only looking at things from a corporate standpoint, not a personal one. It appears I too have many things to learn about the work-life balance.

I go to the refrigerator to pull out a head of lettuce, a couple tomatoes, some red onions, and some large, pitted olives. I grab a large salad bowl and begin chopping up the salad. Finally, I put all the ingredients into a large bowl. As I begin preparing the mixture, Jessica slowly opens the door to her room and is walking over to the kitchen table. However, she is standing away from our kitchen island where I am preparing the salad. Jessica is slowly positioning herself on one of the stools at the kitchen table. I am a bit uncomfortable as she is staring at me. It's amazing how you observe things that you don't usually pay attention to, when so many things are going on around you. It's just me and Jessica in the kitchen.

I look at Jessica and reach my hand out for her to come over and talk to me. "Jessica, what's wrong? You can tell mommy what you are thinking. You can tell me anything and I will always be here to listen. I know you are a very smart little girl, and I also know that you are five years old. I want you to know that you can tell me anything. Talk to me please, Jessica."

Jessica is now looking at me. Her face is reddening, and her little body begins to tremble. Tears begin streaming from her eyes. "Mommy, I love you so much and I don't want to see you die anymore. I am afraid if I help you cook for Daddy, you might forget what you are doing and maybe even who I am."

I immediately stop what I am doing, as emotions are stirring up inside of me. I need to be strong for my daughter. I need to be able to set the stage straight but not lie to her. I need to be authentic. I realize now that I am shaping her core values. This is what she is going to be in life. She has no direction, and she needs direction, despite how smart she is.

I've known a lot of intellectuals out there who thought they were smarter because they were able to figure out analytical problems and excel in mathematics, physics, and science. One prime example is Dr. Fringe. She was a brilliant scientist, but look at what happened to her core values. If she ever had any that were worth noting, I would never have known them from her actions at Medical Solutions.

I stop making the salad at the kitchen island and walk toward Jessica at the kitchen table. We share a kitchen stool with both hands folded on the table. Is this a coincidence? I think not. Jessica is a part of me, and I am a part of her. Our eyes lock together. "Jess, I am not going to lie to you. I don't know if I'll forget what I am doing or for that matter if I will get worse. What I do know is that I love you and that will never change. You must always know the truth and you must always find the truth, no matter what. This is what you must promise me."

Jessica grabs my hand and says, "Mommy, I am scared." I look at Jessica and, with my other hand, I grab her hand. "Jessica, I am scared too. No one knows the future. We need to get through this together. Whatever it is, we are all part of one another, me, you, and Daddy."

Jessica looks at me and begins cracking a smile. My little girl is so beautiful and innocent. Whatever happens to me, affects her. Whatever happens to her affects me. Whatever affects me and her, affects Josh.

I grab Jessica by the hand and bring her over to the island where I am making the salad for dinner. Jessica is a great little helper. We proceed to make the rest of dinner, which comprises roast pork, mashed potatoes, and string beans.

Josh just called on his way home and asked if we wanted to order out, and said he would pick up supper. We told him just to come home and we have a surprise for him.

Josh walks into the house at about 6:30 PM with a briefcase full of paperwork. I tell Josh to wash up and get ready for a meal that Jessica and I prepared especially for him. Josh is dumbfounded. He really doesn't know what to say. I respond to him. "The man of the house is home, and we are your loyal servants, here to serve you dinner." Josh is speechless. He heads upstairs to the bathroom to get ready for dinner and unloads his briefcase in his study.

This is Josh speaking now, for our readers to observe my thoughts.

You just heard Lynn's thoughts and actions. Now it is my turn to open myself up to you, my readers. At present, I am consumed with emotions. I can't believe what I just saw in my daughter and future wife. They prepared dinner for me. This is something I would not have expected in a million years. Lynn and my daughter Jessica have cooked dinner for me! A Co-CEO of Differencia with our daughter serving me, in my house. This is all a dream. I need to be pinched to see if I am awake.

I can't believe that after what Lynn has been through this afternoon, with the news that she is going to share with me tonight, is in such a good mood. She has cooked dinner for me with my daughter assisting! Well, I am going to go along with the uncertainty and see what Lynn is hiding from me, to soften the blow regarding the news she received today. I am now working my way down the stairs and have slipped into something a little bit more comfortable. To me, a little bit more comfortable is a sweatshirt and jeans. Dinner smells delicious. I look over at Jessica and sit at the huge island in the center of our kitchen. I observe that the table is neatly set with the aroma of dinner filling my nostrils. All this is amazing. "Jess, did you cook this all by yourself?" Jessica begins giggling like a typical five-year-old. "No Daddy, Mommy helped me." We all have a hearty laugh together and begin devouring the delicious food sitting before us.

After dinner, the three of us retreat to the dining room to have our chat about the visit with the neurologist and the neuropsychologist this afternoon. We bring Jessica into this conversation because we believe in total transparency between the three of us. In addition, Jessica is smart enough to understand what is going on and has personally observed many of Lynn's symptoms.

Lynn begins the conversation. "Josh, I have good news and I have bad news about my meeting today with the doctors. Do you want me to start with the good news first? Or do you want me to begin with the bad news?" I respond. "I don't have a preference." Jessica remains silent and begins rocking back and forth for comfort, with her legs and arms folded. This is common for her when she gets stressed.

Lynn looks over at Jessica and tells her that if this is too much for her, we can explain this to her later. Jessica nods "no." Lynn continues. "I'll start with the bad news. I might be out of work for the next six months to reduce my stress levels. In fact, I really don't have much of a choice as the doctors recommended that I take time off from the stress I take on, at my job and outside my job."

I look at Lynn and then at Jessica, and sort of give them both a half-smile. You could even think it is closer to a snicker than a smile. "Lynn, let's have the good news that offsets the bad news."

"Josh, I may not have Early-Onset Alzheimer's or dementia. The doctors noted this after extensive blood tests. I have a high amount of a hormone in my blood, that is elevated when I am under extremely stressful conditions, that may cause me to have blackout periods and loss of memory. They figure that if they can reduce my stress levels and retest my blood every couple of months, up to a period of six months, they may be able to clear me to go back to work. In the interim, I can, with minimal stress, help you out as CEO of Differencia." My reaction to Lynn is observed as a nervous laugh. "Josh, are you okay? I don't think I have much of a choice here."

I feel the calm once again. I look over at Lynn sitting across from me and make a move to sit next to her. I signal Jessica to come and sit between the two of us. I reach out and grab both of their hands. "You guys are my family and my life. It took me a long time to really see this through. It is true that everything I do is for you and for those I serve. I need to take responsibility for whatever is to come. I hope that you can trust me to do that."

Suddenly it flashes through my mind, something I learned when I was in grad school that was told to me by one of my economics professors. "This is the first day of the rest of your life." I'm trying to remember his name. What I do remember is that he inspired me, helping me go forward to be successful in life.

Tomorrow, we meet with Dr. Mulcahy at 9:00 AM sharp, to discuss our future at Differencia.

Chapter 9

Lessons Learned

Lynn is home with Jessica awaiting Josh's return from work. She is planning to tell Josh about her meeting with Dr. Pereira and Dr. Friedman.

Lynn asks Jessica if she would like to help her make dinner for Josh.

Jessica retreats to her room and closes the door.

Lynn worries about Jessica's reaction. She muses that true parenting is often very stressful.

Lynn asks Jessica why she is hesitant to help her prepare dinner.

Jessica tells Lynn that she is fearful that Lynn will die.

Lynn muses that she needs to shape her daughter's core values.

Many professionals are so absorbed in their careers that they neglect their core values.

Lynn tells Jessica that she loves her and assures her that she will always tell her the truth.

Jessica indicates that she is scared and that she, Lynn, and Josh must get through the current situation together.

Josh arrives home with a briefcase full of work.

Josh is overjoyed that Lynn and Jessica are preparing dinner for him. He wonders what Lynn will tell him about her meeting with Dr. Pereira and Dr. Friedman.

After dinner, Josh, Lynn, and Jessica go into the dining room to discuss the day's events.

Lynn tells Josh and Jessica that she has some good news and some bad news.

The bad news is that she will be out of full-time work for the next six months. The good news is that she may not have Early-Onset Alzheimer's disease. Lynn reports that if they can reduce her stress levels over the next six months, she may be cleared to return to work.

Josh responds by saying that he will take responsibility, both professionally and personally, going forward.

He realizes that today is the first day of the rest of his life.

Questions to Ponder

Is Jessica's reaction to Lynn's request to help her prepare dinner for Josh reasonable? Why or why not?

Should Lynn be worried about Jessica's reaction? Why or why not? Would you be worried?

How would you have responded to Jessica's reaction?

How can Lynn shape Jessica's core values?

How can you shape the core values of your siblings?

Were you surprised by Jessica's assertion that she, Lynn, and Josh must face the future together? Have your siblings ever expressed this assertion to you?

Do you agree with Lynn's report on the meeting with Dr. Pereira and Dr. Friedman? Would you have reported differently?

Does Lynn's good news outweigh her bad news? Do you think she can reduce her stress levels over the next six months?

In your past, have you properly assessed the good news and bad news aspects of events in your life?

Based upon his past behavior, do you think that Josh will take responsibility for both his professional and personal life going forward?

Given your past failures, do you see tomorrow as "the first day of the rest of your life"?

Key Leadership Qualities Identified

Vulnerability - Capable of being emotionally wounded. Accepting bad news and developing approaches to overcome uncertainty. Many cancer patients accept their diagnosis and resolve to overcome their adversity.

Empathy - Understanding and vicariously experiencing the feelings and thoughts of others. This allows us to develop approaches to assist others in accomplishing their personal and professional goals.

Core Values - Basic principles that motivate behavior. They are the moral compass one follows daily. The core values of first responders are to preserve and promote the health of individuals they meet.

Teamwork - Recognizing that we are all part of a collective effort. There is no "I" in team. Having trust that others will do their part in facing challenges.

Balanced Thinking - Realizing that there are numerous sides to every issue. Leaders understand that there are both positive and negative aspects associated with any decision.

Future Orientation - Leaders understand that tomorrow will bring new opportunities to try new approaches to today's challenges. In the case of Alzheimer's disease, science can look ahead to new medicines and therapies, which can slowdown and/or cure the disease. **Of all the words that have ever been said, the saddest are these: "It might have been."**

Chapter 10
April 27th, 2022, The Day of Reckoning

For our readers, Lynn, and I (Josh) will put our thoughts not verbalized with the characters in this narrative without quotations. Our dialogs as well as all other characters participating in this chapter will have quotations.

It is April 27th at 7:30 AM. Lynn and I just dropped Jessica off at school. I have a million thoughts going through my head and I do not even know how to start a conversation with Lynn as we are driving to Dr. Mulcahy's office. My palate is dry. My right hand is crunched between my seatbelt and my right pocket. I am a mess.

I should be composed and supportive of Lynn. Her life, Jessica's life, my life is in the collective balance of our fates, in one morning meeting with the Board of Directors. There is nothing wrong in being human. Our humanity is tested every day. New challenges arise, seen or unseen, which we as leaders must face. I need to stop thinking of myself.

Lynn glances over to me and calmly says, "Josh, please stop the car and pull over to the curb. I need to have a quick chat with you right now." I have no clue what is fueling this abrupt behavior. Lynn has never been this critical of me. I am sensing in her voice and demeanor that she is serious, and what she has to say cannot wait.

I stop the car and pull over as directed. It is now 7:55 AM, and we have plenty of time to get to Dr. Mulcahy's office. I thought we could stop for a little breakfast and chat about what we are going to say to Dr. Mulcahy before we get to her office. Lynn tells me to shut off the engine. Her face suddenly reddens, and her eyes immediately well up with tears. She grabs both my hands and says softly and gently in a very monotone manner, "Josh, I cannot marry you right now. I need time to think about it. There is too much going on in our lives and I must make a strong case for keeping business as business. I need to separate our personal lives from our professional lives."

I stare at Lynn in horror and dismay. My pulse is racing. My hands are trembling. I don't know how to respond or even where to begin to ask Lynn why she is saying this to me now. I am utterly speechless. My legs feel like jelly. I feel just like somebody shot me right through the heart. I immediately pull my hands away from Lynn and turn my head toward the glass, surrounding the left door of my vehicle. I have no words with which to respond back to her, and don't even know if I'm capable of driving after I start the engine.

Both Lynn and I remain silent for five minutes. I turn in Lynn's direction and say to her, "Lynn, I love you more than anything in this world other than Jessica. Why are you telling me this now, in such a crucial time in our lives? Why couldn't you tell me last night? Why did you wait until we were on our way to see Dr. Mulcahy to decide our collective fates with Differencia? What were you thinking Lynn? What were you thinking?"

Lynn responds softly and gently once again. "Josh, here again it's always about you, isn't it? It was about you today. I was missing and we were supposed to make the announcement of the new drug to the world. You folded under the pressure of everything going on around you. You couldn't think clearly, and you neglected to contact the people in the company who report to you, to tell them what was going on in real time."

My mind is racing at this point. However, something is different. I am not getting angry. I am thinking that Lynn is right. How could I marry her now and take on the responsibility of taking care of her and Jessica, should she become incapable of returning to her job, or even taking care of herself and her daughter? I am thinking that Lynn is merely setting me up for our conversation with Dr. Mulcahy and helping me think out-of-the-box, without the additional burden of taking care of my family and running Differencia. The Board would literally eat me up alive.

Lynn's justification in not marrying me is anything but a personal attack on our fidelity and love for each other and our daughter. For the first time in my life, I am seeing clearer because I am not focusing on my needs. True love is not solely restricted to a legal document that joins two people for life, in a structured ceremony. True love is the respect and trust that two people have for each other through good and bad times.

"Lynn, when you think you are ready to marry me, I will always be there waiting for you. I will do my best to earn your trust, to make our relationship more than a planned partnership that is celebrated by corporate success and profit. Rather, it will be something to be celebrated because of an incredible connection between three people, who have proved unconditional love for one another when facing most dire circumstances.”

Lynn grabs both my hands as we gaze into each other’s eyes. At this moment, I am feeling complete and utter love for Lynn. Our spirits have touched and have melted into one. Whatever challenges we face, we will figure it out, all three of us.

I start the RAV4 and head over to Dr. Mulcahy’s office. I am now realizing for the first time that although Differencia will be a part of our lives, it will not be the dominant force in our existence. I must realize that what we do is make changes in the lives of those who, without medication, would not survive. We are contributing to the mission and goals of Differencia. However, for better or for worse, Differencia will enlighten our existence, not dictate it. Family will always be first.

After our brief encounter on the side of the road, we arrive at the headquarters of Differencia. We enter Dr. Mulcahy’s office at 9:00 AM sharp. She has not arrived yet. Lynn says, “I wonder where she is?” I shrug my shoulders. “I’m sure she’ll be back soon.” The next thing I know, Dr. Mulcahy walks into the office with danishes and coffee for all of us, just the way we like it. She does have a photographic memory and remembered our breakfast orders from our last meeting.

Lynn and I are nervous, and Dr. Mulcahy is calm. She is in a great mood. She gestures to us to have breakfast. We begin with casual conversation prior to walking to her conference table. We seat ourselves and take a deep breath, prior to sharing Lynn's medical condition. We begin to map our collective roles in Differencia going forward. This dialog continues for twenty minutes. We discuss a strategic plan that maps out a strategy to convince the Board that we are ready to take the next step in this new company.

Dr. Mulcahy, after listening attentively without interruption, now speaks. "Lynn and Josh, you are a team sharing the same motives, ideals, and objectives for the promotion of profitable and purposeful enterprise, to enhance the quality of life of otherwise very sick and possibly terminal individuals. This mission could not be fulfilled without your services. Do you agree?"

Lynn doesn't move a muscle in her body. I nod my head affirmatively that I agree with Dr. Mulcahy. Lynn surprisingly snaps at Dr. Mulcahy. "Bonnie, I have been holding this in for too long. I need to be honest with you about myself, as I was honest with Josh this morning. I don't know if I can continue my role as Co-CEO of this company, knowing my present medical situation. I am afraid, Bonnie, for myself, my family, and everyone I am responsible for when I make decisions in this company."

This is Lynn, sharing my inner thoughts with you, our readers. I can't believe what I just said to Dr. Mulcahy. I think I threw Josh under the bus and let him hang out to dry, because of my fears that manifested themselves in this most precarious manner. I have always been known to be professional and on top of things. I am treating myself like an invalid, doomed to die from dementia in a very short period. I have never been like this before, or have reacted this way, under the direst of situations. If this is the new me, I hate it!

Dr. Mulcahy is remaining silent and does not respond to me after my brief outburst. However, she does appear to be glancing at Josh for some type of a response. I am puzzled as to why she is not responding to me and looking at Josh. His hands are folded, lying flat on the conference table and neatly centered in front of him. He appears calm and unflustered. It looks like he is ready to address Dr. Mulcahy, as he looks in her direction while she is looking in his.

"Dr. Mulcahy, Lynn and I, as you know, have been through an incredible ordeal over the past year and a half. It is no secret that we have gone through several trials and tribulations. However, we have persevered. What has gotten us through everything is our faith in each other, and our spiritual consciousness that does not define us necessarily as religious zealots. Religion is structured, accountable, and consequential. Faith is hope, understanding, and does not require anything of physical resources. The only requirement of faith is love." Lynn is looking over at me as the tears are falling from her eyes. I have never seen her this way, at least not in the presence of anybody else, unless she was provoked. She appears to be looking to me for strength, as I have been looking to her all the years I've known her. This is my time to take the lead.

Dr. Mulcahy remains pensive for a moment. "Exactly what are you trying to tell me, Josh? I am not sure what faith or religion has to do with any of our conversation this morning. I thought we were here to talk about the role you and Lynn will play with Differencia going forward. Can you get to the point? Please, I have a very busy agenda with the Board and the future of our company."

I now begin to feel the adrenaline flowing through my body. However, this is my moment in time to prove to her and Lynn that I can be a leader and up for the job. I realize that I can't go into my usual emotional tirades to make a point or get me out of a problem area. I need to be accountable and back up what I just said. Therefore, I am going to make my case right now.

"Dr. Mulcahy, I trust that you have read Lynn's medical report, which I personally hand delivered to you last week."

"Yes, Josh. I have read the report over quite thoroughly, and then took additional time to make sure I got all the important points regarding Lynn's medical condition. I also read the consequences if she does not return to a normal mental capacity for performing her job duties, after a timeline of six months."

I continue. "Dr. Mulcahy, Lynn and I both agreed that she would mentor me in the six-month period that she is away from her job, so that her stress levels can be monitored and see if they are attributed to her dementia." I look to Dr Mulcahy, and I could feel the blood rushing to my head as my adrenaline begins to flow. Once again, I observe my hands. They are still centered calmly on top of the conference room table. This is so unlike me under these types of situations, where I am put in a tight spot and must reply immediately.

"Dr. Mulcahy, nobody knows the future, and I can't sit here and promise you that things will turn up as well as we would like them to. However, I can promise you that the three of us will try to get through all this together as best we can and hope for the best."

"Josh, I serve at the pleasure of the Board of Directors. I strive every day to do what is right for this organization. Hence, I don't need your affirmation that you will try your best and hope for the best. Our organization, although having strong core values, must remain profitable to be competitive with others in our industry. What you have just shared with me does not make this organization profitable, nor satisfy our shareholders who are looking for returns on their investments."

I am ready to respond to Dr. Mulcahy. However, she continues her remarks. "I am not insensitive, nor do I lack empathy for what you and Lynn have been through and are presently going through. These are dire times for all of us. Remember what I said earlier: we are a team. A team must be accountable to one another and accountable to the people that they serve."

I feel my pulse racing as Dr. Mulcahy continues. "The ideology you present for defining the leadership teams delineating the future successes of this company is not built on whims and aspirations. Rather, our strategic plan must be focused on succession and not regression. This is the only language our shareholders will understand, if we want future support to promote our products and services."

I am speechless at this point, and don't know what to say to Dr. Mulcahy in response. This is a side of her that I've never seen, nor do I want to see it again. However, she is speaking the truth, and this is the reality of where we are at this moment. I am trying to put my thoughts together as Lynn slams the conference table with her left hand. This grabs everybody's attention at this meeting. "Bonnie, Josh and I have just poured our hearts out to you. You have my detailed medical report from Dr. Pereira that has been validated by three neuropsychologists. I handed it to you in a sealed envelope."

Dr. Mulcahy remained silent, as I do, and Lynn continues. "I am appalled of your reminding us of our fiduciary obligations to this organization, when we have risked our lives and given 100% of our devotion to rebuilding this organization."

I try to step in to say something, but Lynn shuts me down immediately and tells me to let her continue. "I almost lost my life because of a mistake in the emergency room at the Los Angeles Medical Center.

I took a pseudo-seizure that was mistaken for a stroke. And, to put the frosting on the cake, the pseudo-seizure I took was the result of an argument I had with the totally corrupt Chair of the Board of Directors of our prior company, Dr. Fringe, who we later discovered turned out to be a psychopath. Don't you think we've had enough?"

Dr. Mulcahy chimes in. "Lynn, why don't we just hashtag this entire organization and blast it all over social media! You are acting the same way Josh did when he found out you were missing. He didn't even call one person in the company to tell them what was going on. Who was he protecting, Lynn?"

Lynn responds harshly. "Bonnie, you don't get it, do you? Your life is so consumed with this organization that you don't see the better part of why we do everything we do here. We are trying to preserve the quality of life for people who are less fortunate. You may be the Board of Directors Chairperson, but you are totally oblivious to everything around you, if you accomplish the goals and tasks of this organization to your satisfaction."

Suddenly, the calm returns to me and I respond to both Lynn and Dr. Mulcahy in kind. "Ladies, I am sitting across from the two most important people in my professional and personal lives, absent my most precious possession, my daughter Jessica. You are defending things which are indefensible, yet plausible because you have passion. You both seek to do things that benefit many, unselfishly and unconditionally. However, you are missing the point."

Dr. Mulcahy and Lynn remain silent and listen to words coming out of my mouth that they have never heard from me before. They look at me as if there was another person inside of me that never had a chance to come out and manifest some semblance of true leadership. Honestly, I can't believe what's coming out of me as well, but I want to continue. This is my one moment in time.

I remembered when Lynn was in the hospital last year. Jessica and I had stopped at our local pharmacy to buy Lynn a get-well card. When we approached our car, I noticed the broken mirror and cracked glass on my passenger side. I saw the note left by Mary Wilson, a special needs child with autism, who admitted side swiping my vehicle. The note she left was somewhat incoherent and difficult to decipher. I remember being so angry and lashing out at Jessica for having compassion about the person who did the damage to my vehicle. At the time, Jessica had just turned five years old. I didn't know she tested at genius level. What I did know was that she had feelings and compassion for others.

I remember Jessica lashing out at me when I went on a tirade, yelling about how inconsiderate and careless the person was that sideswiped my car. I remember talking about how it affected me and Jessica lashing out at me. It was something that I could never believe a little girl of five could do. She said, "Daddy, it's always about you. It's never about anybody else." I vaguely remember her words and I know that she did the same thing when we left the hospital after learning about

Lynn's medical condition. This was a child I never knew could come out with a very special leadership skill and take charge of even her father's emotions with determination and confidence.

I continue to address Dr. Mulcahy and Lynn, after the thoughts I just shared with you above, what went through my head in a period of less than one minute. Dr. Mulcahy said after the one-minute time lapse had passed, "Josh, do you need a moment, or do you have something else you want to say?" I responded affirmatively that I wanted to continue.

"I have known Lynn since 2013, and I know her to be a genuine leader, an authentic leader. She not only has passion and commitment to doing the right things at this company. Whatever its present brand, she has a love for life and family that are equally as important. I also share in that commitment. No one has a crystal ball to know what is going to happen in our future. We are all vulnerable to our long- and short-term goals that will affect our balance sheet, positively or negatively."

Dr. Mulcahy remained silent as I continue. "What I do know is that Lynn has been a terrific mentor and mother to our child, Jessica. She has also been a terrific mentor to me. Six months are not going to define this organization's readiness to go forward with a competent CEO or competent Co-CEOs. We all have our jobs to do, domestically and professionally. We make choices in our everyday life, to assess the opportunity cost of every decision that we make."

Dr. Mulcahy is ready to chime in and I put my hand up, to indicate that I am not finished. She continues to yield the floor to me. "Lynn and I have had a serious conversation about what we will do over the next six months as Co-CEOs, in two different venues. She will work from home and continue to mentor me, as she is an experienced CEO. I will continue to work in my present capacity as CEO, while Lynn is away from the office and corporate environment."

I observe that Lynn is beaming at me from ear to ear. Dr. Mulcahy remains silent, yet pensive. She now begins to take notes on what I am saying to her. I continue with our strategic plan. "Lynn and I both agree that if she is experiencing any mental decline over the next six months that inhibits her ability to think clearly and comprehensively and fulfill her duties as Co-CEO, she will resign. I will be the one accepting her resignation and handing it over to you.

Dr. Mulcahy is astonished by the words coming out of my mouth. It was as if she was listening to another person in my place. I continue. "It will be your decision, Dr. Mulcahy, to retain my services or ask for my resignation. I am ready to move forward. Are you?"

Lynn can't suppress her emotions any longer. She looks at me with tears in her eyes and asks Dr. Mulcahy if we could have a moment before we wrap up our session today. Dr. Mulcahy nods affirmatively and tells us she must make a few phone calls in the interim.

Lynn and I exit into the atrium of our corporate office, outside of Dr. Mulcahy's office. We both quietly sit on one of the benches that are surrounded by beautiful rosebushes. The atrium is very much like a greenhouse. Beautiful plants flourish inside, to relax people from taking the heat inside their offices from day-to-day problems that go on in every organization. Lynn looks at me once again as she did earlier this morning and grabs both my hands and states, "Josh, I am so proud of you, and I have every confidence that you will not only provide comfort and support for Jessica and me, but also be a great CEO. One more thing. Yes, I will marry you, and the sooner the better."

Lynn and I return to Dr. Mulcahy's office, and she is waiting for us. She appears to be in the same good mood she was in when she first came in with breakfast two hours ago. Dr. Mulcahy opens the dialogue. "Josh and Lynn, I think I understand where you are both coming from, and you present a very solid case. I think it is one that will work. And, as you stated Josh, no one has a crystal ball and can predict the future. I am on your side, and I believe in the both of you."

Dr. Mulcahy continues, "I had to hear that you were both up to the challenges and the tasks before you. They will be huge and often will put us in some very difficult decision-making scenarios. I put my trust in you that you will do what is right. I am a firm believer that managers do things right and leaders do the right things." Dr. Mulcahy continues. "We will constantly be tested, and we must stick together. I have your back and you have mine, no matter what.

This is my unconditional pledge to you. I will make my case to the Board of Directors and apprise you of their consensus and hopefully their support. You have mine. Now go forth and prosper."

Chapter 10
Lessons Learned

Josh and Lynn drop Jessica off at school and drive to Dr. Mulcahy's office.

Josh muses that he must be supportive of Lynn and Jessica as he begins the next phase of his life.

On the way to Dr. Mulcahy's office, Lynn tells Josh that she cannot marry him right now.

Josh is shocked by Lynn's revelation and asks Lynn how she arrived at this decision.

Lynn repeats her past observation to Josh that he is only concerned with himself.

Josh understands Lynn's concern that he might not be able to care for her and Jessica and lead Differencia at the same time.

Josh recognizes that true relationships are not founded on marriage necessarily, but upon trust and love between two people. He tells Lynn that he will always support her.

Josh continues to drive to Dr. Mulcahy's office, committed to both Differencia and family goals.

Dr. Mulcahy meets Josh and Lynn in her office, and the three of them begin to map out a strategy to lead Differencia. They reaffirm the company's mission statement.

Lynn tells Dr. Mulcahy of her fear that she will not be able to continue in her role as Co-CEO, given her medical condition. She regrets her lack of confidence in Josh's ability to lead Differencia in her absence.

Josh tells Dr. Mulcahy that he and Lynn have successfully overcome challenges in their past, and that through love and trust in each other, they will be able to overcome future challenges.

Dr. Mulcahy indicates that she has read Lynn's medical report and understands the consequences of Lynn not being able to perform her Co-CEO duties after six months.

Josh tells Dr. Mulcahy that he and Lynn have agreed that she will mentor him over the next six months and monitor her stress levels over this time, to assess if her dementia condition has improved.

Dr. Mulcahy tells Josh that Differencia must remain profitable to be competitive with other firms in the industry, and that their strategic plan must focus on succession, not regression.

Lynn chastises Dr. Mulcahy for being insensitive to her plight,t as detailed in her medical report. She tells Dr. Mulcahy that she and Josh have encountered significant setbacks in their past and are ready to move on. She accuses Dr. Mulcahy of being completely obsessed with the goals and objectives of Differencia, and being oblivious to the common good, as described in Differencia's mission statement.

Josh reflects that in his past he was insensitive to Mary Wilson, who swiped his car when he was in the pharmacy to get Jessica a birthday card for Lynn. He recalls he needed to be reminded of this by Jessica, and that he is now sending the same message to Lynn and Dr. Mulcahy.

Josh tells Dr. Mulcahy that Lynn has been a great mentor to him and Jessica, and that they have a plan to lead Differencia over the next six months. Lynn will work from home and mentor him as he continues in his current role as Co-CEO. If Lynn's mental decline over the next six months inhibits her from fulfilling her duties as Co-CEO, she will resign.

Lynn tells Josh that she will marry him and that she has great confidence that he will lead Differencia successfully, and that she will be fully supportive of him and Jessica.

Dr. Mulcahy tells Josh and Lynn that they have her full support in their leading Differencia successfully.

Questions to Ponder

Is Josh over critical of himself in reflecting upon his past behavior? Is he too "backward "thinking?" Explain. Do you dwell too much on the past in your daily thoughts?

What can you do to become more of a "forward" thinker"?

Do you agree with Lynn's initial decision not to marry Josh? Why or why not? Is she being too hyper cautious?

Is Lynn's criticism of Josh for not being attentive to the needs of his employees during the crisis over her medical decision justified? Explain. Have you ever been faced with such a situation in your career?

Do you agree with Josh that trust, love, and respect are the foundations of effective leadership? Can you think of times in your personal and professional lives when love, trust, and respect led to success in overcoming challenges?

Josh reflects that the achievement of family goals should be more important than the achievement of professional goals. Do you agree? In your life, have you placed family goals above personal goals?

What is the source of Lynn's worry that she will not be able to fulfill her duties as Co-CEO of Differencia? Have you ever been faced with a similar medical condition in your past? If so, how did you handle it? What did you learn?

Is Lynn's concern that Josh is not capable of leading Differencia justified? Explain your answer. Have you ever had a similar feeling about some of your employees? How did you handle the situation? Looking back, should you have handled it differently?

Dr. Mulcahy tells Josh that the major goal of Differencia is to remain profitable and to be competitive with other firms in the industry. Do you agree? Why or why not? Should this be the prevailing goal of your Company?

Lynn criticizes Dr. Mulcahy for being myopically focused on Differencia's profitability, to the neglect of employees' personal crises. Is this criticism justified? In your career have you been too focused on corporate profitability at the expense of concern for individuals? Explain your answer. How could you have handled it differently?

Have you ever been confronted by a colleague or family member for being insensitive to their plight? If so, was the criticism justified?

Is Josh and Lynn's plan to decide how to proceed with Lynn's future role with Differencia a sound one? Explain. What would you have done differently?

Is Lynn's decision to marry Josh reasonable, based upon Josh's comments to Dr. Mulcahy? Why or why not?

Is Dr. Mulcahy's decision to fully support Josh and Lynn before the Board of Directors a good one?

Key Leadership Qualities Identified

Trust - The belief that others can be relied upon to assist in the attainment of goals. It must be earned.

Love - Affection based upon admiration, benevolence, or common interests. It is a solid foundation for the achievement of leadership goals.

Respect - Worthy of high regard. Recognition of high competence in a particular regard, either in a professional field or as in the embodiment of core values. It usually takes considerable time to develop.

Empathy - Understanding and sensitivity to the feelings, thoughts, and experiences of others. In the words of Dale Carnegie, "putting yourself in the other guy's shoes."

Forward Thinking - Anticipating what will happen next. In the words of the hockey great Wayne Gretzky, "I don't go to where the puck is, I go to where the puck is going to be."

Core Values - Foundational beliefs in one's thinking. The moral compass guiding one's daily actions. True leaders have clear core values.

Family Focus - Placement of family goals ahead of professional goals. True leadership recognizes that strong family relationships are necessary for strong social and professional relationships.

Platinum Rule - "Treat others the way they want to be treated." This is critical in building trust.

Chapter 11
May 6th, 2022, The Keating Spotlight

(Please note that Josh is speaking here)

There's nothing like a fresh glass of orange juice to start the first day of the rest of your life, if that day determines your life's future, domestically and professionally. I have been waiting for this day my whole life, and I'm not in the least bit excited or motivated by its importance. I find this to be somewhat peculiar. One should be pumped when reaching a plateau in life, believing entitlement is earned.

I am the Co-CEO of a company that employs 11,000 individuals globally, and every word I utter on their behalf, every decision that I make, will reflect upon them negatively or positively. What would Lynn do if she was sitting in my seat in the Boardroom facing the Board of Directors? I am sitting in the CEO seat and will be answering the questions the Board is going to ask in her absence. If Lynn is forced to resign because of her illness, and I am asked to stay on as CEO, what would that mean for Lynn, Jessica, and me, professionally and personally?

Lynn and I have been going over the details of what needs to be done at Differencia, since leaving Dr. Mulcahy's office on April 27th. However, I am not as excited as I should be. There is clearly something wrong with me, and I don't know how to address it, given the present environment. Why am I feeling this aloofness? Is it because Lynn isn't here to assist me or give me support?

To our readers: please note that there are 11 members on the Differencia Board of Directors, led by Dr. Bonnie Mulcahy. The rationale behind 11 Board members is that if there is a tie vote among any issues discussed that need to be addressed immediately, given the nature of our business, the Board Chair, Dr. Mulcahy would be able to break the tie. This has been written into the Differencia bylaws, resulting from the two scandals with former company Medical Solutions, Inc., Differencia's predecessor.

The identification of the Board members may be used for future reference as the narrative continues.

1. ***Dr. Bonnie Mulcahy, research scientist and M.D. Board Chair, Differencia, Inc.***

2. *Dr. Michael Creedon is a Board-certified surgeon at the Los Angeles Medical Center. He is a 20-year veteran of the hospital and has won several awards and distinctions for developing a new technique for open heart bypass surgery.*

3. *Dr. Brent Furan is a Board-certified neuropsychologist, specializing in diseases of the mind, which include Alzheimer's and post-traumatic disorders.*

4. *Mr. Jesse Finkelstein is a real estate developer who helped build two wings of the Los Angeles Medical Center, specifically for the treatment of patients suffering from Alzheimer's disease and dementia-related diseases. Dr. Finkelstein lost his Dad to Alzheimer's in 1982.*

5. *Dr. Craig Foster is a Board-certified pharmacist and philanthropist, whose Dad was one of the founders of Medical Solutions, Inc., the predecessor of Differencia.*

6. *Mr. Fletcher Dixon is an architect who helped design and build three terminals at the LAX airport. His company's name is Dixon and Redmond Architectural Firm, Inc. Brooke Redmond is also a founding partner of the firm.*

7. *Dr. Lynn Ann Marconi, Co-CEO of Differencia, Inc. and former CEO of Medical Solutions, Inc.*

8. *Dr. Bridget West is a Ph.D. in the field of education, and is currently a consultant to the Los Angeles County K-12 school system.*

9. *Dr. Ingrid Frost is a Board-certified chemist, specializing in research and development of new drugs specifically addressing Parkinson's disease and diseases of the thyroid. She has been a consultant to several pharmaceutical companies in the greater Los Angeles area.*

10. *Dr. Marcia Gibson is a general practitioner who practices medicine in her private practice near the Los Angeles Medical Center. Dr. Gibson's father was a philanthropist and a building developer here in the local area.*

11. *Joseph Mondo, Esq. is a senior partner and founder of Mondo Attorneys at Law, who employ over 300 attorneys and partners servicing Los Angeles, San Bernardino, and Modoc counties.*

Dr. Mulcahy and I had met one hour before we got into this Boardroom. We reviewed all of the details of what we're going to talk about, and have collaborated with Lynn since our meeting on April 27th.

The Board members are now assembling, and I am sitting in the Boardroom, representing Differencia, senior staff, and 11,000 employees. Dr. Mulcahy takes her seat with the other Board members as the meeting is beginning to take shape at 10:00 AM sharp. Dr. Mulcahy bangs her gavel on the rubber pad sitting on the huge conference room desk, and promptly opens the meeting.

Dr. Mulcahy respectfully asks for cell phones to be silenced and full attention be given to this very important meeting that will begin to shape the future of Differencia. The minutes from the last meeting have been read. Dr. Mulcahy officially introduces me as the new Co-CEO of Differencia. Dr. Mulcahy asks the Board to officially vote on my new role in the Company. This is only a formality. However, the vote needs to be taken to be official.

In a turn of events, the vote is taken, and the ballots are read. The vote is 5 yeas and five nays. Dr. Mulcahy doesn't vote until all the ballots are in, as written in the bylaws. This really makes me very nervous, as I thought this was going to be a "slam-dunk." Dr. Mulcahy now must cast the tiebreaker. This puts an enormous amount of pressure on Dr. Mulcahy, and this vote will collectively decide my fate going forward by ballot count.

Dr. Mulcahy asked the Board to give her a 15-minute recess with me, before she casts her vote. I thought this to be quite bizarre. However, nevertheless, this was her request, and it needs to be honored. I am now much less aloof and more focused on my purpose of being at this meeting and giving it to the Board straight of what I'm all about.

My problem is not with the Board, but with Dr. Mulcahy. I don't like this cat and mouse situation. Dr. Mulcahy told me she was going to give me her full support when we went into that Board meeting. This vote was only supposed to be a formality and nothing more. It was my understanding that she had already spoken with the Board, and this would be a done deal. Hence, we need to move forward. This is clearly not the case. I feel I am being left at the altar alone, since my bride has walked out on me. I am a consummate failure and being played like a ping-pong ball among a group of deceptive, piranha-eating sharks who could not care less about family, our company, except for their own power. Oh boy, here I go again playing the victim like I always do, whenever I am confronted with a major challenge. I must stop doing this if I am going to do what I promised to do and bring this company forward.

Lynn was right and so was Jessica, that it is always about me not caring about anybody else. This is exactly what I am accusing the Board of doing. How hypocritical I am and how defensive. When everything is going well, I want to take the credit. When things are not going so well, I want to place blame on somebody else, because

I did the right thing, and they didn't. Who needs that type of leader, especially the top leader in the company?

Dr. Mulcahy walks me into her office, which is not far from the main conference room at Differencia. My hands are visibly shaking, and I could feel myself beginning to perspire from nervousness and some major anxiety. I really am trying to relax and stay focused, but it is very difficult.

Dr. Mulcahy opens the conversation by saying to me, "Josh, I know that Lynn is not here to defend you or even enjoin you in this very crucial part of your collective careers. However, based on the vote taken by the Board, there is clearly a much different state of mind since I discussed with you and Lynn being Co-CEOs in this new company." I begin to speak, but Dr. Mulcahy signals to me that she wants to continue. "They clearly knew just how much you and Lynn invested in this new company. Also, they clearly understood that you would be working with Lynn over the next six months to get this new company off the ground. They agreed to all this Josh and, I don't know what happened."

I rebut Dr. Mulcahy's comments. "Either five of them have lost their minds, or some new information could have surfaced about Lynn or me, in between the time you talked to them and today's vote." Dr. Mulcahy responds. "I really don't know the answer to that, Josh. I can't imagine any of that happening, since we seem to have a solid transparency between the Board members. They are all good people. Josh, I vetted them very carefully before we formed this solid group of 11 members." I respond, "Dr. Mulcahy, you have to cast your vote based on what you think is best for Differencia." I feel the calm returning to me. I am focused and there isn't anything in our conversation that will make me waiver from what I am about to say. I feel Lynn strengthens me and I feel my daughter's presence cheering me on as she did when Lynn was in the hospital. We prayed together, not knowing whether she would make it through the night.

We continue the conversation. "Dr. Mulcahy, your vote isn't about me or Lynn. Your vote is about fulfilling the dream the three of us had together, of producing life-saving drugs and making them affordable to people who are less fortunate, who need our science and technology to survive." Dr. Mulcahy begins to speak, and I signal to her that I want to continue.

"Bonnie, we don't have much time before we go back into that Boardroom. I am only going to say this once to you. Lynn and I will find a way to survive and support the needs of our daughter Jessica, as well. We will continue our life's mission to help people, through modern medicine and technology, to deliver a better quality of life." Dr. Mulcahy continues to listen. "I started in this business over a decade ago, as a finance and accounting officer for a Boston based company, and then moved on to what was Medical Solutions, Inc. I then met Lynn Ann Marconi, who has taught me so much about life and about myself. We had a child together because of the love we felt for each other, and for the work that we did."

Dr. Mulcahy signals me to continue. "We both started as financial people in our companies, and we saw how money affects the outcomes of business planning and eventual expansion, leading to high profitability. There is nothing wrong with that. It is economic capitalism and is what keeps our company going and makes us competitive with everyone else that does what we do." Dr. Mulcahy still remains silent as I continue.

"However, just like I felt in that Boardroom today, something was missing. I will tell you what was missing. What we do goes far beyond money. I realize that when we die, we can't take that money with us. All we can do is build a legacy on the good that we have done, to help others that can't get the healthcare they need because they can't afford it. We realized that only people who could afford life-saving medications, through incredible science breakthroughs and technology, would be able to survive the most treacherous types of diseases." Dr. Mulcahy looks at her watch and tells me we have five more minutes before we go back into the Boardroom, where she must cast her deciding vote.

"Dr. Mulcahy, my future wife is risking her life. Working from home and mentoring me will undoubtedly increase her stress levels. She may never be able to return to work full time. I will have the burden of keeping this company moving forward, while taking care of my future wife and my daughter. I will do that, and if that is not good enough, you can have my resignation. I will continue to find a way to survive, and continue the lifework that Lynn and I set up to do. I don't have to remind you that that is why we set up Differencia. I am done. Let's go back into that Boardroom. The die has been cast, and your vote will be the one that counts. Your choice, Dr. Mulcahy!"

Dr. Mulcahy doesn't say a word and stands up, and we walk together through the conference room doors. She bangs her gavel on the rubber pad lying on the conference room table, and asks that the entire vote be retaken once again, after the Board deliberations have ended. I have been asked to leave the Boardroom, but they will call me in when the vote is complete, and the results counted.

I leave the room and immediately call Lynn. She answers the phone and asks me if everything is okay. I explained the whole situation to her and what has transpired.

These are Lynn's words to me: "Josh, whatever the outcome, just know Jessica and I are behind you 100%. This will never change Josh. I can promise you that."

I am filling up with emotion while trying to keep my composure. Lynn, after a brief pause, says to me, "Josh, how would you like to get married on May 22nd?" Suddenly I am speechless. Lynn continues. "My sister Mary is planning the whole thing. Guess who our flower child will be? More to come!" At this moment, not even the Board vote surpasses this feeling of exuberant joy and bliss I am experiencing. My response to Lynn is, "Some little munchkin named Jessica?" Lynn begins laughing hysterically as Dr. Mulcahy opens the conference room doors and signals me to come in to hear the outcome of the vote. She asks the company's recordkeeper to officially record the vote count. The vote count is 11 yeas (Lynn's vote was by proxy) and 0 nays!

I ask Dr. Mulcahy, after the Board is adjourned, why the vote altered so drastically. She explains that my conversation with her was shared with the Board, and any doubt they had in my ability to take over as CEO was relinquished. She further explained that their respect for her and confidence in her abilities to be a competent Board director was sufficient to change their vote. Dr. Mulcahy looks at me as we leave her office and says, "Like I said Josh, they are good people. Don't let me down. Now go home and plan your wedding and come in tomorrow and start running this company. I'm sick of being a babysitter!"

Chapter 11 Lessons Learned

Josh leaves Starbucks after meeting with Dr. Fringe. He thinks about Lynn's position, about the stock deal with Jonathan Peters, and whether she should be accountable for her actions.

Upon driving home, Josh recognizes that he and Lynn have a lot of catching up to do. He muses that business decisions are mostly predicated on the benefits of the few and not on the many.

Josh questions the ethics of Lynn's relationship with Jonathan Peters, and keeping it secretive from the Medical Solutions Board of Directors.

From a philosophical standpoint, Josh recognizes that his <u>Leadership Gene</u> has a long way to go for him to become an authentic leader. He regrets not spending enough time with Lynn and Jessica because of his overwhelming career involvement.

Josh recognizes his responsibility to Jessica, and the need to guide her as she is growing up. He realizes that authentic leaders put others first and themselves last.

Upon returning home, Josh thinks about his relationship with Lynn, Jessica, and Mary, and how important it is to improve these relationships.

Josh reflects that both he and Lynn did not recognize the opportunity cost of being with family. They both were career-centered at the expense of family life.

To be an authentic leader, you need to love yourself first and love your family as you love yourself. You need to share your passions with those around you.

Questions to Ponder

Was the arrangement that Lynn made with Jonathan Peters ethically justified? Why or why not? Have you ever been involved in such a situation?

Have you been neglecting your personal needs in pursuit of your work goals? If so, in what ways? Please be specific.

Do you believe that leaders today are more concerned with their personal gain rather than the common good?

Do you have a leadership gene? What is it? Is it based in ancestry, environment, habit?

Can your leadership gene be improved? If so, how?

Do you take responsibility for your offspring(s) success? How do you accomplish this? In what ways can you improve?

Authentic leaders learn from their mistakes. What are some of the serious mistakes you have made in your life? What did you learn? Have you modified your behavior as a result?

Do you have any mentors in your life? What have you learned from them? Have they helped you define your core values?

How important to you are your family and extended family relationships? How can they be improved? Are you grateful for your interpersonal relationships? In what ways are you grateful?

It takes years of practice to become an authentic leader. What practices do you engage in to improve your leadership skills?

It is often said that spending "quality time with others is a substitute for quantity time". Do you believe this to be true?

The authentic leader believes that love of self and family is the essential building block for success in life. Do you agree? How can you increase your love of self and love of family?

Key Leadership Qualities Identified

Ethics - Doing what is right by following core principles. If it doesn't feel right, it isn't right. Follow your moral compass.

Self-Care - Taking care of oneself is essential in helping others to achieve their goals. Authentic leaders must have physical and mental health, to have the energy to help others become the best version of themselves.

Leadership Gene - This encompasses the leadership qualities which are part of one's character. They are based upon ancestry, environment, and character.

Learning from Failures - Authentic leaders learn from their mistakes. They get up every time they fall. They never lose. They view challenges and failures as learning experiences. This makes them stronger when facing future challenges.

Gratitude - Be grateful for your strengths and successes. This will make you optimistic in your outlook and drive you to be proactive rather than reactive.

Success - Success is a continuous process. "The road to success is always under construction." Obstacles encountered along life's journey are viewed as "bumps" in the road.

Forgiveness - Authentic leaders are always willing to forgive. They realize that resentment is negative and poisonous and inhibits them from being focused on achieving their personal and professional goals. They constantly strive to strengthen their relationships with others.

Chapter 12
May 13th, 2022, Truth or Consequences

"What will it be, Josh? Do you want the first chair at this all-day Board meeting, which will start in fifteen minutes? Or do you want me to go through my agenda for the first half of the meeting, and you can go on right after our lunch break? As Co-CEO, and given Lynn's physical absence on campus here, it's your call."

A nervous feeling is coming over me. I don't know how to respond. Dr. Mulcahy is looking at me and begins to chuckle. "Josh, this isn't a death sentence. It is merely a rhetorical question as a matter of protocol." I loosen up. "Sorry Bonnie. I have never represented an entire company going before the company's Board of Directors. I guess I'm a little nervous."

Dr. Mulcahy responds to me. "I have my focus Josh. You have your agenda. Are you the CEO or not? I can no longer babysit you. We need to move forward and have a huge agenda!"

I realize that the future of this Company is based on my ability to move forward. I laid out my strategic plan to Dr. Mulcahy on May 6th as Co-CEO. She had my back then and still has it now. She has confidence in my ability to run this Company. I need to get over myself and move forward. "Bonnie, I would prefer to go into the meeting and present to the Board my assessment, following your opening remarks and the reading of the minutes."

"Sounds like a plan, Josh. We've gone over your agenda, and I would like you to present it in the order that you gave it to me. The Board can follow on their agenda copies." I smile at Dr. Mulcahy and begin walking into the conference room with her, as I open my agenda items to address at this meeting, which I will share with my readers.

1) *Introduce myself as the new acting CEO and Co-CEO of Differencia.*

2) *Address the historical significance of transitioning Medical Solutions, Inc. into a new corporate enterprise, Differencia.*

3) *Provide a logistical validation of a new vision for the new corporation.*

4) *Introduce corporate leadership's vision, mission, and working methodological order.*

5) *Take questions from Board members.*

6) *Yield the meeting to Dr. Mulcahy's agenda.*

Entering the Board meeting room, I take my seat next to Dr. Mulcahy. All members have a copy of my agenda and focus on opening remarks. Dr. Mulcahy formally opens the meeting and bangs her gavel on the rubber pad resting on the glass, centered over a massive mahogany table which seats all the Board members, Dr. Mulcahy and myself. There is a transcriber in the room to electronically take the meeting minutes. I am somewhat intimidated by my surroundings while looking up at the polarized glass roof of the conference room and the beautiful, hand-crafted, marble circular supporting beams surrounding the room.

The Boardroom chairs are designed for total comfort, and their coverings are hand-woven Corinthian leather. I think they probably cost anywhere from $750-$1,000 each. No expense was spared to put this conference room together. Looking around this room gives me a feeling of power and money. However, here I am in a room where decisions are made that ultimately affect the health and well-being of hundreds of thousands of people around the globe and over 11,000 employees.

All this is flashing through my head while Dr. Mulcahy reviews her agenda for today's session. We have such a long way to go to make Differencia a reality for the wealthy and upper-middle-class individuals who can afford the drugs that we make, and those entitled to a quality of care that sustains life, if it is feasible to be maintained with our new drugs. I don't know if this is possible in the next two years, five years, twenty years, or ever. I understand that this is the vision Lynn and I have set for this Company, this new Company we call Differencia.

Dr. Mulcahy asks if I am ready to move forward with my opening remarks to the Board of Directors. I nod to Dr. Mulcahy in the affirmative, take a sip of water, clear my throat with my hand over my mouth, and smile at everyone. The following words to come out of my mouth are, "Good morning, Dear Board Members." The Board members return my greeting with a resounding, "Good morning." At least this makes me feel good and welcome.

Here I go. Wish me luck! "I would first like to thank you for your vote of confidence in approving my new position at Differencia as Co-CEO and acting CEO, in Lynn's physical absence." There is silence at this point, and all eyes are on me. I take another sip of water and clear my throat once again. Dr. Mulcahy is looking at me to say, keep this moving. I continue. "I realize that a total restructuring of the former Medical Solutions, Inc. took almost a year of painstaking, necessary changes to create our new organization, Differencia, which means in Latin, to make a difference."

I continue. "We have, over the past decade, experienced two major scandals in the former company, Medical Solutions, Inc., which no longer exists. However, we cannot put our past in hiding. We must remember what brought this Company down and drove it to get up again and keep functioning with a brand-new vision, mission, and strategic plan. Each step of this exercise was reviewed by you, the Board members, and approved by Lynn. What we do going forward will affect the lives of over 11,000 Differencia employees, and hundreds of thousands of people who receive our drugs and benefit from them."

I take another sip of water and carefully choose my words. "As you know, the ethics committee vetted many of the Board members before the panel sitting before me was approved, so that we could retain our core values and continue to make progress in our primary mission. This mission is based on the vision our predecessor, Medical Solutions, Inc., defined almost three decades ago." Dr. Mulcahy clears her throat and signals me to slow down.

I continue. "We will not flaunt that mission, but rather embellish it. Our mantra will be to provide medicines that will heal the sick, and generically tailor them through our research with ingredients that will be affordable to as many needed recipients as possible."

Dr. Mulcahy looks up at me once again with a very concerned look on her face. She bangs her gavel and asks the Board to take a 15-minute recess and have some refreshments before we continue. She signals it will be a very long day, and small reasonable breaks between the plan would keep us refreshed and focused.

Dr. Mulcahy and I walk out of the Conference room together and sit on one of the benches in the atrium of the corporate building. She opens our conversation by stating the following. "Josh, where are you going with this? You must use your words carefully as you speak before the entire Board of Directors. It would be best if you were careful how you posture yourself, as every word that you say is translated into what they're thinking on how they will address our shareholders at the next shareholders meeting. These people invest in our company and give us the resources to research, manufacture, and market the products that make us competitive with other industries."

I look at Dr. Mulcahy and can't even begin to get the words out of my mouth. I am so afraid that they might disturb her or make her feel uneasy. She wants me to be strong. She wants me to be the CEO, and at the same time, she wants me to lighten the load on my delivery, to appease the Board of Directors because they need to address the shareholders and don't want to upset them. Am I missing something here? Is my role here to play politics with the new vision of our Company? All I have done so far is introduce myself and build the foundation to deliver our new vision. This is everything Lynn, Bonnie, and I talked about over the past several months.

I respond, "Dr. Mulcahy, you want me to be a CEO, present our vision that we've worked on for months on end, and at the same time appease the Board of Director,s so that they might be able to play politics with the investors that fund our programs? Is that correct, Dr. Mulcahy?"

She responds sharply back to me. "Do you want me to be a babysitter again, Josh?" I can feel the adrenaline running through my body as the anger begins to mount, and I think I need Lynn next to me right now, telling me how I should handle the situation. She was once a CEO. She had to deal with Dr. Fringe. She faced up to Dr. Fringe and refused to put a drug on the market that the FDA did not clear because incomplete data was presented for their review, and she could not have that. Her conscience wouldn't allow her to compromise her core principles. So, what am I doing here right now arguing with this person who may be going down the same path as Dr. Fringe? Or is she?

This Parkinson's drug is her baby now. She is no longer the second fiddle to Dr. Fringe. She is the Chair of the Board of Directors. Every word that comes out of her mouth means something. She has a new role, as I do. I need to return to her with a good response and then return to the meeting and do my job. My follow-up response to Dr. Mulcahy is going to be direct and final. It's her choice. I have just about come to the end of my rope with this Company, and here is where I sink or swim.

"Dr. Mulcahy, I am the Co-CEO of this new company, Differencia. In Lynn's absence, I am the acting CEO. I want to get one thing straight. You are not my babysitter. You are not my parent. Outside of the realm of your office as Chair of the Board of Directors, you are a department head and one of my employees for whom I am responsible." Dr. Mulcahy takes a deep breath as I continue my statement to her, before we walk back into the Boardroom.

"Lynn continues to be a Board member and a Co-CEO. I am not a Board member. My twofold role in this Company is to act on behalf of the people that we serve, to improve the quality of life in their very existence. Secondly, I am responsible for the 11,000 plus employees I consider my internal customers. This includes you, Dr. Mulcahy." She is looking at me with benevolence and respect and I feel like a Chief Operating Officer in this company. Dr. Mulcahy responsed back to me, "Mr. CEO, let's get back into the Boardroom."

I walk into the Boardroom with Dr. Mulcahy, and she signals me over to the catering station, set up inside the two brass doors of our conference room. It is almost 11:00, and we don't break for lunch until 1:00 PM. This is my opportunity to sell my vision to the Board with our newly formed Company, Differencia. I am energized and ready to take the next step in moving our vision forward. I believe once I accomplish getting our vision into the heads of the Board members, we can move forward and begin a discussion about the new mission. I can move on to Q&A, which will end my agenda for the day.

Dr. Mulcahy bangs her gavel and opens the next session of our Board meeting. Her agenda begins right after lunch. I am scheduled for another two hours, to make my presentation and then open the floor with the Board for questions and answers. I hope to complete this process before Dr. Mulcahy begins her agenda, which will complete the entire day's session with the Board.

I continue my presentation. "Dear Board members, I hope you enjoyed your refreshments during our small break. I want you to know that I had a few minutes to think about some of the points I had shared with you about our vision. I would like to continue with our new revised mission statement."

Dr. Mulcahy continues to look at me intently, suggesting "don't screw up, Josh." I glance at her. I feel the calm entering my body again, and Lynn's strength inside me for some strange reason. The only thing that I can think of now, which supersedes the pressure of what I am about to say to the Board, will be to marry Lynn ten days from now. This is the focus of my life. Therefore, I am doing all this. I am doing this for me, Lynn, Jessica, and everyone in my charge. If this is not good enough, I guess it's too bad. Isn't it?

I continue my report to the Board. "I am one person who represents many other people, inside and outside this Company. However, my jurisdiction is based on your empowerment of my actions, and not the other way around. I don't pretend. I have never been a political person. I am basically, as many of you would characterize in more colloquial terms, 'a bean counter.' "

"Since I entered this business more than a decade and a half ago, my job was to make sure that I could maximize the profitability of every department that I worked in. I did not have the opportunity, nor the inclination to look beyond that role that I played for so many years, until I met Dr. Lynn Ann Marconi, my future wife; and watched the birth of my daughter Jessica, which awakened my thirst to become an authentic leader."

Dr. Mulcahy continues to look at me with more respect and less skepticism. "I honestly thought that the only thing that could motivate me was money. I honestly thought that the goal of making money was to make more money. I honestly thought that maximizing the profit of the company should be my only goal, until I discovered that leadership was lacking, and sustainability was necessary."

Dr. Mulcahy is again looking at me in a very concerned manner. "My Dear Board Members, I want to share what changed my mind and led me to the vision and mission statement I will present to you in the next thirty minutes. This vision will represent the purpose of our new Company, and why I chose to stay with Differencia and not leave, after all the scandals that we have been through with Medical Solutions over the past decade. I did this because I want to make a difference and save my family's dignity and the 11,000 families of our employees that we service." Dr. Mulcahy is now taking off her glasses and rubbing her eyes, and meticulously returning her glasses to her face as I continue.

"The vision of this newly founded company is to make a difference in the quality of lives for so many, who would otherwise perish without our products. We have a Parkinson's drug that can cure so many people. However, not many people can afford the drug, and would live a much lower quality of life and even perish a lot sooner without it. The drug testing, as you know, has not yet been completed, and is still not ready to be presented to the FDA."

Dr. Mulcahy takes another look at me and signals me to move on as her agenda is almost ready to take over, as we are closing in on the lunch break. I take another sip of water and get ready to continue my presentation to the Board. However, I notice that you could hear a pin drop, and I have the Board's undivided attention. Dr. Mulcahy makes the same observation, and I am ready to continue when one of the Board members interrupts.

Dr. Ingrid Frost is a Board-certified chemist, who specializes in researching and developing new drugs, specifically Parkinson's and thyroid drugs. She had consulted with several pharmaceutical companies in the Los Angeles area, including Differencia, then Medical Solutions, when it existed. She does not sit on any other Boards in the pharma industry, as that would represent a conflict of interests.

Dr. Frost fires off her first question. She was born and raised in Australia and migrated to the United States when she was eleven years old. She settled in Boston with her family. She holds an M.D. specializing in Neurology, and a Ph.D. in Chemical and Biological Sciences. She is 46 years of age and works as a pharmaceutical consultant and chemist with one of the major pharmaceutical companies in the Boston area. *For purposes of this narrative, these companies and characters mentioned in this narrative are fictional.*

"Mr. Keating, your vision statement for this newly formed organization you call Differencia, is to make a difference in the quality of lives for so many, who would otherwise perish without our products.' Do you have substantiated proof that your Parkinson's drug, as it presently stands, will make a difference in the quality of lives of individuals who would not survive without access to our drugs?"

I clear my throat and look over at Dr. Mulcahy, who doesn't say a word; and Lynn is not here to answer the question. This is all up to me now. I can feel the adrenaline flowing through my body. I am at a loss for words, because my statement was made based on an assumption of the research that our Company had completed, under the direction of Dr. Mulcahy and her predecessor, Dr. Fringe. I would have to go back to them to answer this question, in addition to presenting complex data to back up my assumptions. If I am to be an authentic leader, I must tell her the truth: that I don't know the answer. However, on the other hand, I could lose my credibility as a CEO if I don't give her a solution or the answer she is looking for.

I look over at Dr. Mulcahy, and she gives me a blank stare, like the one Lynn gave me. I observed her writing down some notes on a legal-size pad of paper and cleaning her eyeglasses, as she and all the other Board members awaited my answer to Dr. Frost.

"Dr. Frost, as the new acting CEO of this organization, my focus is to create a vision for Differencia, and not get bogged down in the details of the research that backs the statement I just made." I am ready to continue, and Dr. Frost immediately interrupts me. "Mr. Keating, you are sitting here with eleven Board members listening to you, looking for answers to justify this new organization and put us on the map as a miracle drug maker. This will generate hundreds of millions of dollars of revenue. Is this correct? You are saying to me then that you haven't got a clue of how to defend our continued existence with hard data on the drugs we produce, thus promoting the game changers of the century?"

As much as I am trying to stay calm, I feel myself beginning to sweat profusely. I have a hole in my rowboat and nothing to plug it up. I am sinking very quickly. I have two choices. My first choice is to admit that I don't know how to answer Dr. Frost's question. My second choice is to defer the question to Dr. Mulcahy, which will seal my fate with this organization as a CEO or any other position. In my relationship with Lynn, I realized that she was never a quitter and always told the truth. I continue with Dr. Frost. This will be my quote-unquote Hail Mary pass.

Suddenly the calm returns to me, and I stop sweating and shaking. I remember listening to a song long ago, sung by the late Whitney Houston, entitled "The Greatest Love of All." I also remember some of the words in that song, which are now standing out in my head and resounding in the beautiful voice of Whitney Houston. These are the words: "If I fail, if I succeed, at least I'll live as I believe. No matter what they take from me, they can't take away my dignity. Because the greatest love is happening to me. The greatest love of all inside of me."

My head is spinning out of control in a nexus of complete contentment. The reason is the greatest love inside of me is Lynn. I have searched for this love my whole life, and I am the winner here. As much as I love my job, I love Lynn above everything in this world, except for my daughter Jessica, who is the product of the love Lynn and I share for each other. This is too precious to give up on a question. The words sung by Whitney Houston make sense to me now. I am ready to answer Dr. Frost's question.

"Dr. Frost, I am a new CEO with this newly formed Company. This is the company that all the Board members who presently remain with this organization voted on. Additionally, you voted me into this position unanimously. If memory serves me correctly, you have entrusted me with the forward progression of this organization, what it stands for, and what resources it will need to turn that vision and mission statement into a viable strategic plan that makes us competitive."

Dr. Frost remains silent and allows me to continue, as Dr. Mulcahy continues to take notes. "I was unprepared to answer your question, and I refuse to give you an answer that will jeopardize me and anyone else in this Company. Your question needs to be researched. Today, my job was to deliver a newfound possibility, to offer hope to so many, through the decades of research we have performed in this Company, old and new, to make a difference in peoples' lives. I do not pretend to be a scientist. However, I know about finance and how to make this organization profitable."

Dr. Mulcahy continues her blank stare at me and continues to take notes. "Dr. Frost, I mean no disrespect, and I will research every avenue tirelessly and efficiently, to make this new company successful and to accomplish its vision and its mission. Our new mission will drive our strategic plan. This mission will allow us to utilize the resources within our reach to make affordable drugs, so that people can improve their quality of life; who are bedridden and devastated with disease. I want to start with Parkinson's. I understand this is your expertise."

Dr. Frost looks up at me and speaks. "Mr. Keating, I just have one more question for you." I look over at Dr. Mulcahy, give Dr. Frost a quick chuckle and shake my head. My response is: "I am all ears." Dr. Frost smiles in a more benevolent than snide manner. "Mr. Keating, how do you propose we maintain our profit margins, to satisfy the investors that provide us the resources that we need to make the so-called affordable drugs, to everyone that needs them?"

I put my head down, and think for a minute. I look over at Dr. Frost, and my responses are as follows. "Dr. Frost, not too long ago, I looked at my partner and Co-CEO, Dr. Lynn Ann Marconi, ready to get her head sliced open because of a medical error. I thought I was going to lose her forever. I watched a little girl, not much older than Jessica, have the life sucked out of her because of Covid; and there was nothing anybody could do to save her. Her parents did all the right things, and they seemed to be able to afford her care."

I observed Dr. Frost's face getting very red and noticeably disturbed by my comments. I continue. "Dr. Frost, can you imagine what it would be like to see that little girl pull through Covid? Can you imagine what it would be like to share our wealth and leave a legacy behind, because we made a difference in a medical breakthrough for many grateful individuals who would be able to remain alive from our efforts? "

Dr. Frost looks at me, shakes her head, and states: "Josh, you have so much to learn about how this business works. I do not condemn people because of their status. I do not feel sorry for people because of their status. I am a chemist that makes drugs and makes recommendations to pharmaceutical companies, to improve the quality of life of individuals. I don't decide the prices. This Company is only focused on one thing, making people well. Just remember that before you criticize us. Sometimes we must sacrifice to get a result. And we can't choose who lives and who dies."

Dr. Mulcahy finally bangs the gavel, and we break for lunch. We leave the conference room to return to her office for a debriefing of our first meeting. She looks at me and speaks. "Josh, go home, and on your way home, buy a bottle of wine and celebrate your first meeting as CEO. Tell Lynn she's got a future husband she should be very proud of, in his first meeting as CEO.

"I will continue my meeting with the Board, and we will meet soon to prepare for our next step. Good luck tomorrow, when you sit in the corner office and run your new company. Remember, I am your loyal employee and will get some of the answers in my department, asked by Dr. Frost, and report back to you so you can be prepared for the next step! We will turn those assumptions into a reality."

Chapter 12 Lessons Learned

Dr. Mulcahy asks Josh if he wishes to be placed first on the Board meeting agenda.

Josh feels uneasy about being first on the agenda.

Dr. McKay expresses displeasure over Josh's hesitancy to move forward in addressing the Board.

Upon reflection, Josh agrees to open the meeting with remarks to the Board.

Josh introduces himself as the new acting CEO and Co-CEO of Differencia.

Before making his remarks to the Board, Josh muses that his mission is to make investors profitable and to make lifesaving drugs available to the general population, irrespective of their wealth.

Josh explains to the Board the reasons for restructuring the former Medical Solutions, and the formation of the new Company called Differencia.

Josh pledges to the Board his actions as Co-CEO and acting CEO will be to make Differencia more profitable and to make its lifesaving drugs affordable to the general population.

Dr. Mulcahy tells the Board that she would like to take a 15-minute recess.

She indicates to Josh the importance of conveying to the Board his ability to successfully lead Differencia in successfully accomplishing his vision.

Josh questions Dr. Mulcahy's motives. Is she compromising her core principles, as Dr. Fringe did?

Josh responds to Dr. Mulcahy that he is responsible to Differencia's 11,000 plus employees and improving the quality of life of those suffering from serious life-threatening illnesses, and by providing these lifesaving drugs to the general population at an affordable cost.

Dr. Mulcahy and Josh reenter the Boardroom and schedule 2 hours to make his presentation and address Board members.

In his presentation, Josh tells the Board that his main mission is always to maximize the profitability of every department he has worked in. He reflects that in his view of his role was to be too myopic and needs to expand into the area of social welfare.

The new mission statement and strategic plan must expand to include producing lifesaving drugs for everyone at an affordable cost.

Joshua receives a question from Dr. Ingrid Frost, a Board-certified chemist. She asks if Josh has substantial proof that Differencia's Parkinson's drug will make a difference in the quality of life of individuals who would not survive without the drug.

Why is Josh uneasy about being placed first on the agenda? Is it because he lacks confidence in himself or because he is not prepared? Preparation improves self-confidence. Do you prepare for presentations you need to make? If so, how do you prepare?

Should Differencia's major objective be to increase its profitability, or to advance the common good? What is your Company's major objective? Do you agree with its major objective?

Do you agree with Differencia's mission statement, that its purpose is to increase profitability and to make lifesaving drugs affordable to the general population?

Is Dr. Mulcahy too overwhelming in coaching Josh for his Board presentation? Should she express more confidence in him? Have you had a superior in your past who treated you in this way? What effect did it have on you?

Is Josh's response to Dr. Mulcahy an effective response? Why or why not?

Is Josh's response to Dr. Mulcahy an effective response? Why or why not?

Should Josh have been prepared for Dr. Frost's question concerning his not having knowledge of research supporting the effectiveness of the Company's life-saving drug? Does your Company have supporting evidence indicating that it can deliver on its mission statement? Dr. Frost believes that Differencia must be principally concerned with profitability, and that in the short run, other goals such as the production of lifesaving drugs at an affordable cost must be sacrificed. Do you agree with this? Has your Company ever been faced with such a situation?

If you were to describe Dr. Frost's mission statement, what would it be? Please describe the mission statement of the best superior you ever had.

Key Leadership Qualities Identified

Preparation - Remaining focused on the message to be delivered. Having contingency plans for what might happen. When driving, it is leaving sufficient room between your car and the cars around you.

Constructive Criticism - Pointing out to others how they respond to a situation can be improved. It concentrates on an individual's actions and not the individual themselves.

Branding - Clear transparency as to what a Company stands for. This is key to developing trust in a successful relationship with consumers.

Clairvoyance - The ability to gain information about an object or person through extrasensory perception. Successful leaders possess this ability to anticipate unexpected developments.

Pareto Optimality - No one can be made better off without someone else being made worse off. This involves the optimal tradeoff between profitability and the promotion of the common good.

Chapter 13

May 22nd, 2022, The Wedding

The trip to the altar has not been easy. However, the decision to go to the altar was based on benevolence and trust. It took from 2013 to the present day to go through this exercise called "verify and trust."

Together, Lynn and I have been through some tough times. However, most of that time was fruitful and rewarding. We learned how to trust each other. We learned how to pray together. We learned about our honorable deeds and our wrongdoings, past and present. We watched our lives erode and rise from the bowels of hell to the brink of total jubilation, calmness, and ecstasy. We realized that trust, transparency, and connectedness are more than words. To some, these words are meaningless acronyms for pseudo-epistemology, leading to deception and mistrust. To others, these words translate into absolute authenticity and commitment to self and to whom we serve.

Jessica is not only our child, but a life commitment between us. Jessica is much more than the result of a business relationship that turned into a personal commitment. She is the sole reason that justifies our passion for creating Differencia. Neither Jessica nor Differencia can ever be compromised. To clarify, this does not mean that we compare the value of Jessica to Differencia. It is quite the contrary. Both require our undivided attention for different reasons.

Our child, Jessica, does not require any validation for unconditional commitmen,t nor any justification for unconditional love from us.

This commitment does not and will never require proof of that love from anything or anyone. On the other hand, Differencia requires commitment from its 11,000 employees, those that support it, and those that provide the resources to keep it vibrant and competitive to support its vision and mission.

It is now Thursday, May 19th, 2022, two days before our wedding, and I have never seen Lynn so radiant and glowing as she is today. I asked myself, how can a business relationship turn into such a beautiful commitment between two individuals? Before meeting Lynn, I had dated several women who were extremely intelligent, attractive, and committed to starting a relationship with me. I am going back to when I looked at personal relationships as noncommittal with business. Instead, I viewed business as a business and personal relationships as what they were, separate from business relationships. What makes our relationship different? If you know the answer to that, you are a better person than I. The two should never mix.

Here we are getting ready to stand at the altar, and I have not a clue to give answers to what I have shared with my readers and the paragraphs preceding this one. I find it quite ironic that thirty years from now, as I write my memoirs, I will be asking the same questions, yet to produce an answer.

This evening, we have invited our pastor from Immaculate Conception Church in downtown Los Angeles, Msgr. Michael McLaughlin for dinner. He has been a close friend of my family since I moved to

LA. He has baptized Jessica and has given me several lectures on the sacrament of marriage, which had gone in one ear and out the other since Jessica was a baby. Now, his wishes will be coming to fruition.

This evening, Msgr. McLaughlin will be going over the dress rehearsal for our wedding on May 22nd, following last Sunday's Mass at noon. Our ceremony will be in Immaculate Conception Church at 1:00 PM. The guests at the wedding were by invitation only, notified, and have accepted their invitations. There will be one hundred guests of family, coworkers, and friends. The dress rehearsal will be tomorrow.

Our wedding party will include Mary Wilson, one of Jessica's best friends, although there is a stark difference in their ages. Joan Wilson, Mary's mother, Mary Marconi, Lynn's sister, Dr. Bonnie Mulcahy, Chair of the Board of Directors at Differencia, and Jonathan Peters, former CEO of Medical Solutions, Inc., now Differencia, will also be part of the wedding party. Mary, Lynn's sister, will be Lynn's maid of honor. I have chosen Jonathan Peters to be my best man. The flower child will be Mary Wilson, Jessica's best friend, and Jessica will be the ring bearer. All members of the Board of Directors have been invited, and a few of the shareholders not to be named for purposes of this narrative.

We are not getting a caterer for Msgr. McLaughlin's dinner this evening. Instead, Lynn and Jessica are going to make dinner. They will prepare homemade lasagna, accompanied by a rigorous and robust vegetable salad, which will be served after cheese and crackers. In all the years I have known Lynn, I have never seen this domestic side of her. It is impressive to watch her and her daughter work together and make a beautiful meal. Lynn and Jessica are singing their childhood songs, including "The Itsy-Bitsy Spider." Lynn remembers all the words and is not missing a beat in the dialogue, and the movements of her hands and feet and her executive functioning seem perfect. In fact, I am observing the Lynn I have known for so many years, which fills me with joy.

It is now 4:45 PM, and Msgr. McLaughlin will be here at 6:00. One thing I know about him is that he is never late for anything. He is a stickler for performing his tasks and duties on time, and is meticulous and efficient about what he delivers. I would say that he is a true leader in our huge parish in downtown Los Angeles. When he speaks to his congregation, especially during Mass, it is as if he is talking to each parishioner individually, in a church that holds up to three hundred people during services. Msgr. McLaughlin is a true leader. He inspires others to do things ethically and promotes total transparency. He tells us he will never interfere with our personal lives and that our choices have consequences, all of them. He tells us that God forgives us, no matter how great the sin, if we genuinely repent and agree not to sin again.

I always wanted to believe that no one could tell me what to do unless I wanted to do it. This is part of what makes me authentic. Although I may have made mistakes many times in my life, I can always rectify my actions and turn over a new leaf. Much of this philosophy came from Msgr. McLaughlin. In many ways, I think that you can learn how to be a leader. However, I still firmly believe that you must have a strong passion or desire to lead, in addition to inside influences. This is not to say that I am right. I think this to be true. I cannot prove it. However, I can validate it by my actions.

It is now almost 5:45 PM, and I help Lynn and Jessica set the table for the Msgr.'s visit. He does not know what to expect when he walks in. Jessica is very fond of the Monsignor because he always tells her a story when he comes over to the house, or we visit the parish rectory to drop off some clothes for a local charity. It is now 6:00 and I hear the doorbell ring. As always, the Msgr. is right on time. Jessica runs to the door and greets him. Jessica is intrigued by his Roman collar and his black suit. Because he is a Msgr., he has a thin red piece of fabric inside his collar, signifying his status in the Roman Catholic church. He brings in a freshly baked lemon meringue pie (one of Lynn's favorites) and a beautiful bouquet of red roses for our dining room table.

I tell him that Lynn and I will be getting ready to serve dinner in about fifteen minutes, and he is free to relax in our spacious dining room. We will call him when dinner is ready. Lynn puts the cheese and crackers on the glass coffee table with our friend's known preferred drink of choice, Chardonnay. Msgr. McLaughlin smiles and graciously takes his glass of wine and walks into the dining room to relax a bit.

Msgr. McLaughlin asks Jessica if she would like to keep him company while Lynn and I set the main dining room table for dinner. I cannot help but overhear Jessica's conversation with him. In the middle of the conversation, I hear Jessica ask a strange but interesting question. "Msgr. McLaughlin, when mommy was sick and we thought she was going to die, we went to the hospital, and they told us she was going to get better. They made a mistake on what was wrong with her."

I observe a little girl who tests at genius levels, but speaks like a five-year-old when she addresses this issue about her mother. She is not speaking the way she has been speaking over the past year. It is different. She is talking like a child, not a mental giant with an IQ of almost 150. Msgr. McLaughlin gives Jessica his full attention. He responds, "Please continue, child." Jessica continues. "Daddy and I found out later that mommy would be all right."

 "Well, that was a good thing, Jessica, wasn't it?" Jessica responds. "I don't know why the little girl we saw in the hospital, who was as old as me, was probably going to die. God did not save her." The tears begin rolling down Jessica's face as her face reddens. When she gets stressed, she folds her arms and rocks back and forth at rapid intervals. She continues in a loud screeching tone. "Why did God make mommy live and make that little girl die? It's not fair. It's not fair." The tears continued to roll down Jessica's face, and her tiny hands tremble as she continues. "I love Mommy, and I do not want her to die. I am happy she didn't die. I don't want to live if she dies, or Daddy dies!" Jessica screeches out again, "Why does God choose who lives and dies, when he can save everybody who deserves to live?"

Msgr. McLaughlin grabs Jessica by both hands and pulls her into his arms. He kisses her forehead and tries to console her as she whimpers softly. In a soft tone, he tells Jessica the following. "Jessica, two days ago, I was at the St. Jude's Children's Hospital. There were babies and small children who were suffering from cancer. Some of these children were going to get better, and some will not get better. I tried to make their parents feel better, but it was hard. I have been a priest for many years. My job is to make people feel better."

I looked at my daughter, and I looked at Msgr. McLaughlin trying to console her. He continued. "Jessica, God's plan is not always our plan of what we want. God's plan is a mystery that no one can understand, because we are not God. Jesus was dying on the cross, and he asked his Father why he did not save him from such a terrible death.

"If you believe that Jesus was God and his Father could not save Him, how can I answer your question? I do not know Jessica. When we die, we will know. We must accept what God wants us to accept and continue to believe that we will find medicine and doctors to save people like that little girl you saw in the hospital."

At this point, Lynn and I are filled with emotion. This conversation with the Msgr. and my daughter has comforted me for some reason. This conversation has given me hope to fight as hard as possible to make this Parkinson's drug and all the other drugs that we develop at Differencia a reality for as many people as possible. It will be a lengthy battle with the Board of Directors and shareholders to accomplish our vision and mission. However, this battle is worth fighting. This conversation has given me renewed energy.

We finally sit down and have our dinner. The conversation we have just heard did not continue for the rest of the evening. We shared a lot of laughter, preparation for the dress rehearsal tomorrow, some good stories, and reminiscing old times in our parish that made us feel like we were on top of the world. As far as this evening is concerned, Lynn, Jessica, and I learned a lot from Msgr. McLaughlin about what authenticity is all about. He was very transparent with Jessica. He was direct but very gentle. He told her in not so many words that he asked the same questions. He did not make up a story and try to justify and speak for God's actions.

Msgr. McLaughlin shared the fact that we are all human. Our religion tells us that Jesus was both God and man. Whatever you want to believe, the lesson to be learned is that we do not always have the answers. However, whether we think there is a higher power or not that decides whether people live or die, our connectedness to one another translates into synergistic energy that gives us hope to continue to create opportunities that will help cure diseases of the body, mind, and spirit. Two days after tomorrow is the wedding. We are ready to go forward.

It is Friday, May 20th. It is two days before our wedding. Lynn and I have decided to write individual vows to one another and not share them until we recite them in our wedding ceremony. Our daughter Jessica asked if she could say something to Lynn and me during the ceremony after exchanging our vows. We asked Monsignor McLaughlin if it was okay. He knows Jessica's intelligence level and her commitment to Lynn and me. He approved. He asked her if she had written her words down, so he could look at them before she shared them at the ceremony. Jessica told him that the words were in her heart and that she did not need to write them down. He accepted her explanation and we moved on to finish our dinner.

Lynn and I have decided to postpone our honeymoon until we get Differencia up and rolling. The dress rehearsal is at 11:00 AM and we have just finished breakfast. It's almost 10:00 AM. Thankfully, Immaculate Conception is only a few minutes away from our townhouse. I have yet to hire a new Director of Operations. This will be our priority next week, after the wedding.

It is now 10:45 AM, and Lynn, Jessica, and I get into our SUV and proceed to Immaculate Conception Church. Once we get there, we will wait for the rest of our wedding party to arrive. We arrive at 11:10 AM and Msgr. McLaughlin is waiting for us. Lynn greets him with a big "Hello!" He gestures for Lynn and me to approach the altar, asking Jessica if she would kindly sit in the first pew for a couple of minutes until he talks to Mommy and Daddy. Jessica giggles and smiles at Msgr. from ear to ear. He approaches the first pew and settles Jessica into her iPad without any distraction.

Msgr. McLaughlin opens the dialogue as follows, speaking in an exceptionally soft and serious tone. "Josh and Lynn, you both know how fond I am of you and your daughter, Jessica. However, I have been recently taking a lot of heat from my superior, Bishop Ronald J. Mulcahy." I immediately respond to him by addressing the question to my future wife. "Lynn, could I just be imagining this, but is it possible that Bishop Mulcahy is related to Dr. Bonnie Mulcahy? Please tell me this is not the case."

Without hesitation, Msgr. McLaughlin responds by looking at us and stating, "Bishop Mulcahy is Bonnie Mulcahy's older brother. He was ordained at St. Joseph's seminary, located in downtown LA, and received his Master of Theology at UCLA, followed by a Doctor of Theology at Harvard University. He has been ordained an auxiliary bishop in the district of Arlington Heights in Los Angeles County in 2014 and one of the youngest bishops ever to serve in Los Angeles County."

I respond to Msgr. McLaughlin. "But all due respect, Msgr., why are you taking heat from Bishop Mulcahy? Is it because you are officiating in our wedding on May 22nd?" I then turn to Lynn. "Lynn, did you know Bishop Mulcahy and Bonnie Mulcahy were brother and sister?" Without hesitation, Lynn responds back to me. "Josh, we made a pact to have no secrets, and I kept my promise. I had absolutely no idea until now that they were related. Bonnie has never said anything to me."

I told Lynn that I believed her and asked Msgr. McLaughlin to continue discussing the alleged heat he was taking from Bishop Mulcahy for officiating at our ceremony, that's coming up in two days. Jessica is now beginning to get a little fidgety in the first pew. I ask him to move it along and get to the point in a very discrete manner.

Msgr. McLaughlin continues. "Josh, the people in my parish are questioning your relationship with Lynn. They know that you both had a plutonic business relationship that resulted in your child's birth. Bishop Mulcahy believes that Jessica was born out of wedlock, and as the result of a business arrangement. Additionally, he has not spoken to his sister Bonnie for over ten years, since she became involved in making and producing drugs priced so expensively that people who cannot afford them end up dying. He thinks what she is doing is amoral."

Lynn and I are looking at Msgr. McLaughlin in shock. I respond to him in kind. "Msgr. McLaughlin, I am not a politician, nor do I pretend to be one! I am appalled that an official of the church I support would go to these extremes to prevent or raise havoc on a business relationship that bloomed into a beautiful family, including my daughter, Jessica. I will not stand here in front of my future wife and daughter, and in the eyes of God, and be intimidated or belittled by a belief or disbelief in our relationship as valid, accountable, and transparent."

Msgr. McLaughlin remained silent as I continued. Just as I am ready to open my mouth, Lynn steps in with the following message. "Msgr., go back to your bishop and tell him that we are not on Earth to judge, but rather to be judged by our actions, reformations, transparencies, and faith in one another. If you choose not to officiate at our ceremony on Sunday, we will continue our lives as we have, until we find a priest that will accept us for who we are and not what they want us to be in their judgments."

Lynn's eyes fill with tears, as they fall down her cheeks and onto her beautiful silk blouse. Lynn continues. "Msgr. McLaughlin, Josh, Jessica, and I are one. We will continue our work to help others who cannot otherwise help themselves sustain life. We are not answering a Gallup poll on how people judge us to succeed at what we do. We are leaders in our field. We are leaders in our home. We are leaders with those that interact with us. Our wishes are to give back to society what we take from them in profits. What say you, Msgr. McLaughlin? Will you perform the ceremony on Sunday or not?"

Msgr. McLaughlin remains silent until he asks Jessica to approach the altar, and reaches his hand out to grab hers. He looks at her and says, "Jessica, you have your mother's eyes and strong will. You have your father's heart and compassion. You will be a beautiful ring bearer at Mom and Dad's wedding. I will be proud to take the rings from you, so that they can place them on each other's fingers." Lynn's eyes fill with tears once again, meeting my joy-filled eyes. The three of us grab hands and reach out to grab Msgr. McLaughlin's hands, forming a big circle. This is our connectedness. This is the leadership in our world, reaching to everybody else's world. This is the synergy that makes authentic leaders "authentic."

We all need to stand up for what is right. We also need to realize that doing the right things may not always be politically correct. Right things can never be challenged. They can only be duplicated. Sometimes they require change that is uncomfortable but often necessary. This relationship feels right because it is right. We are not corporations. We are real people with honest agendas. People set the tone for corporations. It is not the other way around. Standing up for truth, transparency and connectedness stifles righteousness, ignorance, and arrogance. Do not be fooled by the differences.

Saturday, May 21st, was a day of running around on roller skates, ensuring everything was in order. Everything was checked out and verified, from the caterer to the baker who made the cakes to the catering services, the violin music for our ceremony, etc. "Houston, the launch is a go."

It is now the day of our wedding. The morning is filled with taking pictures with all the photographers and the niceties that come with a beautiful day and a beautiful wedding. The Immaculate Conception Church is filled with guests, observers, family, and friends. However, the most essential thing in this church right now is the love Lynn and I feel for each other, which brought us to this plateau. There is nothing more beautiful than a bride who is about to offer her unconditional love to her spouse. I no longer see Lynn as a business partner. I only see her now as my wife. I remember seeing it somewhere in Scripture: "Give Caesar what is Caesar's, and God what is God's." Somehow, this reverberates in my mind as Msgr. McLaughlin blesses our union and directs us to read our wedding vows to each other.

I am asked to go first. Jessica, standing next to Msgr. McLaughlin, stretches her arms for Lynn and me to hold both her hands as we exchange vows. I am on the left, and Lynn is on the right. I go first. "Lynn, you are my life, body, mind, and soul. Although we met ten years ago, I feel you have been my soulmate and always in my life. I do not know how I ever lived without you before we met. I dreaded the moment I realized we might have lost you. I have embraced every moment of my life since I knew you would be with me. I cherish you and our daughter. I want to be with you forever."

I finish my vows with Lynn and quickly observe her face as Jessica continued to hold on to us. It's now Lynn's turn to recite her vows to me. I feel the energy between us and the connectedness of what makes us human, and how we cannot survive without each other. We will always be one, no matter what obstacles we encounter and how difficult they may be.

"Josh, I fell in love with you the first time we walked along the beach, looked into each other's eyes, as the ocean waves caressed our feet in the cool sand of a warm summer night in August a few years back. I never fell in love with my business partner. I fell in love with the soulmate I had been searching for my whole life. You are why I continue, and I will keep fighting, to continue for what we both believe. However, no matter what, I will always believe in you, and I will love you forever."

There is not a dry eye in the church. However, there is one more piece to the ceremony. That piece is my daughter Jessica. She lets go of both our hands, and Msgr. McLaughlin nods his head for her to say the words she has been holding since we spoke at dinner last Thursday evening. "Mom and Dad, I know you love me, but you can never love me as much as I love you. I know that I am smart, and I can't help that I am smart. Smart does not make me love anything. Everybody is smart and does not always do smart things. Mom and Dad, I love you because you are part of me, and I am part of you. When Mommy didn't die, God told me he loved me. He loves me not because I am smart, but because He wanted me to be your daughter. I love you both forever."

Again, not a dry eye in the church. The rest of the day went beautifully, and many lessons were learned in this chapter of our lives. We will remember this day for as long as we live. Despite the challenges we might face and the obstacles we might encounter, we are one. We are connected and will never separate from one another. Someone also once said, "Let no one separate what God has joined together." This is also reverberating in my mind as we walk into our reception.

Today we leave as one. Happy trails to what comes ahead!

Chapter 13
Lessons Learned

Josh realizes that trust, transparency, and connectedness will be necessary to maintain and develop a strong relationship with Lynn, Jessica, and himself.

In his thinking, Josh reflects that Jessica and Differencia must be given equal attention and that one should not be compromised at the expense of the other.

Josh feels both a deep business and personal relationship with Lynn, a relationship unlike any other he has had in his life.

Lynn and Josh invite Monsignor Michael McLaughlin for dinner in preparation for their wedding.

The wedding party will include Joan Wilson (Mary Wilson's mother), Mary Marconi (Lynn's sister), Dr. Mulcahy, and Jonathan Peters (former CEO of Medical Solutions). The flower child will be Mary Wilson and Jessica will be the ring bearer.

Lynn and Jessica prepare dinner while singing childhood songs together.

Josh recognizes Monsignor McLaughlin as a true leader who does things ethically and promotes total transparency. He believes that Monsignor McLaughlin instilled in him the quality of self-forgiveness, a key trait of the authentic leader.

After Monsignor McLaughlin arrives at the house, Jessica asks him why God allowed her mother, Lynn, to live, and made the little girl her age she saw in the hospital die. She asks why God chooses who lives and dies when He can save everybody who deserves to live.

Monsignor McLaughlin tells Jessica that we do not have an answer to that question. He says we must accept what God wants us to accept, and continue to believe that he will find medicines and doctors to save people like the little girl she saw in the hospital.

Josh muses whether there is a higher power that decides whether people live or die. Our connectedness to one another translates into synergistic energy that gives us hope to create opportunities that will cure diseases of the body, mind, and spirit.

Lynn and Josh prepare their wedding vows and Jessica prepares her own remarks to deliver at the wedding.

Lynn and Josh arrive at the Immaculate Conception Church for their wedding ceremony.

Monsignor McLaughlin tells Lynn and Josh that he is "taking heat" from Bishop Mulcahy, the brother of Dr. Bonnie Mulcahy.

Monsignor McLaughlin tells Josh that he learned from Bishop Mulcahy that Jessica was born out of wedlock and was the result of a business arrangement. He asserts that the Bishop believes that his sister Bonnie is involved in making and producing drugs so expensively that people who cannot afford them end up dying. He thinks what she is doing is immoral.

Josh responds with indignation and says he is appalled by Bishop Mulcahy's position and says he will not be intimidated by the accusations. He says he and Lynn should be judged by their actions and faith in one another. He tells Monsignor McLaughlin that if he does not want to officiate in the wedding ceremony, he will find someone else who will.

Monsignor McLaughlin agrees to officiate at the wedding, realizing the strong bond which exists between Josh, Lynn, and Jessica.

The wedding ceremony takes place flawlessly, with Lynn and Josh expressing their never-ending devotion and love for each other.

Jessica tells Lynn and Josh that she loves them because she is part of them, and they are part of her. This is the essence of human connectedness.

Josh concludes his thinking by realizing that leadership is more about connecting people to one another than telling people what to do and trying to control their actions.

Is it possible to have both a deeply personal and business relationship with another person? Do you have a deep business and personal relationship with someone?

What is your assessment of Monsignor McLaughlin? What are his core principles?

What did you think of the dialogue between Monsignor McLaughlin and Jessica? Do you believe that a higher power exists? If so, have you ever asked a higher power why bad things happen to good people? What did you think of the answer Monsignor McLaughlin gave Jessica?

Do you agree with Bishop Mulcahy's assertion that because Jessica was born out of wedlock, in a business arrangement, that Josh and Lynn's characters are flawed?

Do you agree with Bishop Mulcahy's belief that because Dr. Mulcahy is involved in making and producing drugs so expensively that people who cannot afford them end up dying that she is immoral?

In your view, was Josh's response to Bishop Mulcahy's indictment of his and Lynn's moral character persuasive?

Do you agree with Josh's assertion that he and Lynn should be judged by their actions and commitment to each other and Jessica?

Do you believe that true leadership is based upon connectedness and not persuading others of your point of view?

Key Leadership Qualities Identified

Commitment - A pledge to do something in the future. Total dedication to achieving a goal. A good example is Mother Teresa's commitment to eradicating leprosy.

Courage - The choice and willingness to confront agony, pain, danger, uncertainty, or intimidation in pursuit of a goal. President Franklin Roosevelt's commitment to improving public welfare, in the face of his polio, is a case in point.

Justice - The qualities of equity, evenhandedness, fairness, and objectivity in dealing with issues. Authentic leaders bring this perspective to bear in their interactions. Susan B. Anthony brought this quality to bear in securing the rights of women.

Resolve - The firm commitment to pursue a goal, irrespective of the difficulty in achieving it. The US had the resolve to land a man on the moon in the 1960s. Perseverance and unwavering commitment allowed the US to achieve this goal.

Chapter 14

Four Days Before the Board Meeting

It's May 23rd, 2022. I cannot take a day off to recuperate from my wedding. Heck, we were partying until 2:00 AM last night, when we finally said goodbye to our remaining guests. It was the most memorable day of our lives, which it should be. Here I am, back in my office at 8:00 AM. with less than five hours of sleep, and a huge agenda to follow, prepared by my assistant last Friday. The agenda was undersigned by Mary Watkins, Executive Assistant to Acting CEO Joshua Keating. I like the sound of that title. It has a unique ring that I earned over a quarter of a century ago, when I first got into this business. Let me stop gloating all over myself and get to work!

My agenda has over twenty-two items listed that I need to accomplish in the next nine hours. At least, these are the timeslots that my assistant plugged me into, so I could get through most of my meetings. Most importantly, I must meet with Board members individually, on items concerning our Friday meeting at 9:00 AM which is scheduled for the entire day.

My first meeting today is at 9:30 AM, with a candidate who was one of the finalists for the position of Director of Operations, my former position before getting appointed as Co-CEO by the Board of Directors. I remember when I first interviewed for the position of Chief Financial Officer at Medical Solutions with Jonathan Peters, its CEO. I was so nervous that day and I never got a chance to interview in his office. I was late for the appointment, and I could not reschedule.

After a major scandal at Medical Solutions, my wife and business partner, Dr. Lynn Ann Marconi, asked me to be her Director of Operations after she was appointed CEO. I realize that this was almost a decade ago. I am now the Co-CEO of a new Company that spun off from Medical Solutions. I was part of the decision to rename this company, Differencia (meaning to make a difference in Latin).

This has been quite a ride over the past decade. I have made so many mistakes. However, I have learned so much from so many people I cared about, and many that I didn't care about. In learning about myself, I realized that animosities could ruin companies, especially in higher circles. Core values are compromised. Saints turn into sinners, and companies fall apart. We have come a long way to get to where I am sitting today. I realize that it's not about me in this office. Instead, it is the position that I hold in this Company. Anyone could be sitting in my plush leather chair in the corner office. However, those responsible for calling the shots in this corner office may not be accountable for their actions. It depends on what type of leaders the Company chooses to represent its interests and the interests of those they serve. This monologue in my head is shared with you, the reader, to prelude what is to come in this chapter. This will be the beginning of the biggest challenge in my professional career as the acting CEO of Differencia.

I am going through my list of agenda items and getting ready to meet my first chosen finalist applicant for the position of Director of Operations. I get to item number eleven on my agenda items for today, and notice that I am meeting Human Resources at 1:30 PM this afternoon to discuss potential labor cuts, specifically in our Research and Development Department. I don't understand where this is coming from, as I have had no discussions about any labor cuts in any departments with Dr. Mulcahy, Lynn, or any other high-level staff members, specifically in the finance department. The Director of Finance and Chief Financial Officer, Dr. Brody Young, is not on my agenda for today, or before our Board meeting this Friday at 9:00 AM.

At this moment, I am infuriated by what I am reading, and in a state of total confusion. My first impulse is to call Lynn at home. However, she is at a doctor's appointment with Jessica, who has complained about having pain in her ears. She could have an ear infection, and that can be very painful. I don't want to disturb Lynn right now, and besides, I am acting CEO and should be able to handle this staffing problem myself.

I am ready for my 9:30 appointment to interview the first candidate, Mikayla Weinstein, for my former job as Director of Operations. Mikayla is highly personable and comes from a very impressive background. She graduated from Rutgers with an MBA in finance. Her last position was Chief Financial Officer for Proctor, Bowes and Hunch, a financial equities firm with corporate offices in Stanford, Connecticut. She has held that position for the past eight years. I asked Mikayla why she wanted to leave such a secure position, earning an excellent salary with bonus incentives. Following a long pause, Mikayla explained that although her company was a fabulous company for whom she loved working, she wanted to do something with her life that promoted the welfare of the ordinary person, contributing to the greater good.

I told Mikayla that I respected and understood her thinking. However, our base starting salary was substantially less than she made at Proctor, Hutch and Bowes, with bonuses and incentives. Mikayla put her head down while slightly chuckling at my remark. "Mr. Keating, I have made more money than I could have ever dreamed over the past eight years. I work in a fabulous company with fabulous people. My financial team encompassed the most dedicated individuals on the planet. My future financial perspective is more than secure to last me three lifetimes."

Mikayla's face muscles tightened, and she looks at me with the melancholiest expression I had ever seen. "Mr. Keating, my neighbor, Peter Jones, has a four-year-old daughter with Type I Diabetes, and he has Parkinson's disease. Mr. Jones was one of my clients. He put his patent on a new sailboat design that revolutionized the entire sailboat industry. Any manufacturer that made sailboats would be able to sell this design at a premium price to those who could afford it."

I immediately became all ears. This turned out to be no ordinary interview, but a wake-up call to me. I fear where this is leading. My instincts tell me that I must listen to what comes next and what Mikayla must share with me. I feel it in my bones that this leads to a higher calling, which I alone must answer.

I asked Mikayla to continue as she paused to hold back her emotions. Mikayla continues. "Mr. Jones immediately became famous with this new design. He was literally on every boating magazine in the country and even got international recognition for his design. Mr. Keating, Mr. Jones developed this design when he was 34 years old. He earned unimaginable amounts of money and was sitting on top of the world." I remained silent and didn't say a word, and asked Mikayla if she would like a glass of water. Mikayla declined the water and continued her story.

"Mr. Keating, when Mr. Jones was 38 years old, and I was in my fifth year at Proctor, he was diagnosed with Parkinson's disease and, for whatever reason, quickly moved to stage IV of a stage V process. When Mr. Jones reached stage IV, the doctors told him he only had a few more years to enjoy his family. He quickly sold his business and is facing an imminent awful end to his life."

I got up from my seat in my office and asked my assistant if she would get us two bottles of spring water, accompanied by two glasses of ice. I asked Mikayla to continue and somehow lost sight momentarily of why she was in my office in the first place. I am not suffering from dementia, but am absorbed by the content of this very harrowing interview for my former job.

Mikayla continued. "Mr. Keating, financially I am not as well off as Mr. Jones is or was. However, money doesn't impress me as much as being part of something which can cure diseases like Parkinson's. Mr. Keating, I know your drug, if approved by the FDA, can only work in the early stages of Parkinson's. However, I also realize that this will prompt further research to obliterate this disease at any stage."

I respond to Mikayla. "Did you also tell me that Mr. Jones has a daughter with Type I Diabetes?" She responded to me affirmatively and let me know that Mr. Jones could well afford her treatment. However, she showed a vital concern for individuals who couldn't afford insulin because of the high cost. Some may even have lost their lives because they couldn't get the insulin they needed.

The remainder of the interview went well, and I told Mikayla that she was on a short list of finalists, a very short list. We would be getting back to her over the next two weeks, as the Company needed a Director of Operations as soon as possible.

After getting through the first nine items on my agenda, it was 1:05 PM. I decided to have a quick lunch in my office, consisting of green beans, a Cobb salad, and a Diet Coke. I chose to walk down the corporate hall on the third floor of our building and meet with Reese Miles, our HR director. Reese has been with us for almost twenty years. Next to Lynn, I trust Reese more than anyone else I work with in this Company.

I value her opinion greatly, and I know she has always been a straight shooter whenever she was dealing with me. I need to get to the bottom of what is prompting my agenda item to call for changes in our staffing, especially in research and development that oversees getting this Parkinson's drug out in the field as soon as possible and comply with the FDA. We need to make sure that there will be no open-ended questions that prompt the FDA to hold up the drug release once again. We certainly need the revenue to cover our overhead and satisfy our shareholders.

It is a five-minute walk once I get off the elevator to Reese's office. I realize that my schedule only allows thirty-five minutes with her, until I get to my next agenda item. She greets me with open arms, as we have not seen each other since my promotion. She has a spacious office and four assistants supporting HR. Each assistant oversees their specialization and designation.

Reese is aware of our time restraint and gets right to the point. "Josh, the Board of Directors has decided to downsize approximately 20% of the R&D staff. We hired approximately fifty staff scientists to work on the Parkinson's drug over three years ago. As a result of their high salaries, and to remain competitive, we need to downsize after learning that the Parkinson's project has been put on hold until further notice."

Adrenaline was flowing through my body. I could feel my hair standing up on my scalp. My heart was racing, and my hands immediately began to sweat and shake. At this point, my readers are probably thinking I am overreacting to this information. Perhaps I am, not getting all the facts yet. Well, that's just me. I am an emotional person, and my passion is not just to be a CEO and make money, but to drive home the whole reason I come to work here every day. Please just bear with me as I continue this story. I try to remain as calm as possible. However, I find it very difficult to restrain myself after this news. I palm my hands together in repetitive motion and ask the following question to Reese: "Please tell me who decided to put the Parkinson's project on hold until further notice?" She looked at me in utter amazement. "Josh, you mean you didn't know that the project was put on hold?" I respond to her, "Reese, I did not hear or know about the Parkinson's project being put on hold, ever!"

Reese responds. "Josh, you were out of the office a few days last week, and the Board of Directors called me into a meeting they were having. It was an emergency meeting to discuss budgeting and staffing for future projects. They invited me and Dr. Brody Young, the Director of Finance, into the meeting. I would have assumed you knew about this. Therefore, it was on your agenda for today's meeting. They wanted me to discuss this with you."

I respond sharply to her. "Reese, you're telling me after the fact about something I did not know about. The Board went over my head, addressed two of my staff to attend one of their meetings in which the Co-CEOs were not present, because they were getting married, and then decided to cut 20% of my research and development staff without my knowledge. To top it all off, they decide to eliminate a long-standing project Lynn and I have been working on for years and then, put it on hold!"

I hear my voice beginning to escalate as I address Reese, who was silent and oblivious to what was going on with this new company, Differencia. She pauses for a minute, puts her head down, takes off her glasses, and looks up at me. "Josh, did you talk to Lynn or Rodney about this?" I respond to her, "Reese, I had no knowledge of any of this going on until now. Or, when I first looked at the agenda items, that I was going to meet with you today to discuss potential staff cuts."

At this point, I advise her that until I talk to the Board, Lynn, Brody, and Dr. Mulcahy, I am not going to make any suggestions or recommendations for any staff cuts. I also tell her to keep our conversation in confidence, until I get more information about what is going on. As I leave her office, I wonder why the Board would support this type of information from getting to me. Is it that they don't respect my position? Will the stress lead to Lynn starting to forget things again?

I got through my agenda items for the rest of the day, and I arrived home at about 7:30 PM. Jessica has already eaten supper and will be getting ready for bed soon, after doing her little routine with Lynn. This routine involves what Jessica did during the day at school and what new things she learned. Lynn tries to get her to learn one new thing every day. This is also a good exercise for Lynn's memory recall and helps keep her stress levels at a minimum.

Lynn and I sit and have a quiet dinner, while Jessica is playing on her iPad, and will be in bed no later than 8:00 P.M. During the warmer months of the year, we let her stay up a little bit longer so she can spend more time with us, although sometimes Daddy gets home later than expected. This was one of those days.

Lynn and I go through our routine, catch up on our day, and then usually after we eat, we migrate into the dining room to enjoy some after-dinner espresso and good conversation. In the conversation, I prelude a statement of what happened in agenda item number eleven of my day's activities with a nervously projected joke to Lynn. "When I met with Reese Miles today, she told me we were cutting 20% of our R&D staff, because our Parkinson's project was put on hold. This decision was allegedly made by the Board of Directors in an emergency meeting last Saturday, when we were away getting married. I don't know how that's possible, because Dr. Mulcahy was in our wedding party on the day we got married. Don't you think she probably would've mentioned something to us?"

Lynn looks at me and doesn't say a word. I know that look, and it scares the dickens out of me. I respond to the look on her face. "Lynn, I am begging you, please do not tell me you knew about this decision. Please don't tell me that I have been deceived once again.

Please don't tell me that my role as Co-CEO is nothing more than a joke to this company."

Lynn remains silent as the tears start coming down her face as she responds to me. "Josh, I am not going to lie to you and tell you I didn't know about this meeting while we were away getting married. I did not want to spoil our wedding. What we mean to each other is much more precious than any job. I knew how you would react, as you are now once learning this news."

My emotions have peaked, and I feel the blood rushing to my head, to the point where I think I'm going to take a stroke at age 43. I am staring into Lynn's eyes, and time has come to a standstill. My self-worth is related to my ego, which has been reduced to no more than dust floating across concrete pavement in the middle of a busy city street. My closest friend, soulmate, and the mother of my child, did not trust me enough to tell me that the project we had worked on for over two years was put on hold, with no indication of starting up anytime soon with the news of the impending layoff.

I slowly lift myself from my chair, take another look at Lynn, and retreat to Jessica's bedroom to check up on her without saying a word. Lynn asked me if we could continue our conversation after I check on Jessica. I give her no response. I leave Lynn sitting in the dining room, with her head positioned on her lifted knees, resting on the sofa cushions of the two-person loveseat.

I leave Jessica's room and decide to go outside and think a little bit about where I was going next, not only with my job, but with my life. I am still in denial and disbelief, and I have a meeting with Dr. Mulcahy first thing in the morning. I don't even know how to begin with her tomorrow morning. I don't know what to say to my wife and business partner. Somehow, I am reminded that the whole reason why we set up Differencia was to help others who couldn't otherwise help themselves. These were our core values. Why did we default? I need some answers soon!

The calm finally returns as it usually does. If I am to be a CEO, I need to get reasons why I was not informed about putting the Parkinson's drug on hold, and subsequent approval of the decision to lay off 20% of our research and development staff. Although this will kill me, I must go back and talk to Lynn as a business partner and not as an emotional crybaby, whimpering because he heard something he didn't like. Whether that something is justified remains to be seen. However, these questions need to be addressed civilly, unbiased, and unemotionally. I need to approach Lynn not as my wife, but as my business partner, who was responsible for running a Company as CEO before we became Co-CEOs.

I walk inside the house, and I find Lynn in the same position she was in before I walked outside to get some fresh air and clear my head. She summons me to sit next to her on the loveseat in the dining room, grabs me by the hand, and rests my head gently on her lap with the other hand. "Josh, do you think I was out to deceive you?" Lynn states in a very soft voice. "Do you think the most precious possession in my life would be put at risk because of some inherent secret she was trying to keep away from him? You'd better think twice."

I immediately pulled my head from her lap and looked her straight in the eye. "Lynn, what would you expect me to think? You just divulged to me that you had knowledge that the Board decided to put the Parkinson's drug on hold, and I had no input in the decision, nor was I informed of such a decision. I feel like I am the Company mascot, a joke to be reckoned with."

Lynn looks at me and sharply responds. "If that's what you think as Co-CEO of Differencia, which you helped plan and put together, then you are a joke! How dare you say something like that to me. I have fought tooth and nail to give you every accolade and opportunity to bring you to the top of the ladder in a multi-billion-dollar enterprise, and this is how you respond to me?"

I don't think I had ever seen Lynn this mad at me. She was furious at my reaction to the secret she kept from me. She had gone behind my back and voted on a decision that crippled our project and allowed 20% of our staff in research and development to lose their jobs. Many of these people had families. Many of these people had medical issues and were loyal employees for many years at Medical Solutions, then transitioning to Differencia. They would lose their salaries, medical benefits, and vacations.

"So, Lynn, is this why you chose not to tell me anything? Tell me this isn't so. Tell me that you didn't vote on this choice to put the Parkinson's project on hold and lay off 20% of the R&D staff of 50 employees or so?" Lynn remains silent. "Oh, I forgot you were Co-CEO, so you could make that decision without my knowledge, and it would count as a vote with the Board because you are still a Board member. What was the Board count, Lynn? Did they get your vote? I am just curious!" I could hear my voice escalating, but I couldn't control it.

Lynn's eyes begin to fill with tears, and she sharply shouts back to me, "Josh, I almost gave my life for this Company and vowed the rest of my life to you and our daughter, Jessica. Why would you ever think I was trying to deceive you? I am up against a lot of pressure and am trying to balance our relationship with work and personal life. There is no simple way to say this."

I finally shut my mouth and let her continue talking. "Josh, I love you more than I love myself, and only our daughter Jessica comes before the both of us. We are all part of each other. As a member of the Board, I have a fiduciary obligation to vote my conscience when it comes to matters involving our shareholders and investors. You do understand that, right?"

"Lynn, I remember not too long ago, you told me that we were not going to have any secrets between us, both business and professional. Did you not tell me this?" She responds, "Yes, Josh, I remember telling you this, and I intended to tell you tonight before you jumped all over me and started screaming at me for keeping a secret from you." I respond, "What was I supposed to say, Lynn, under the circumstances? If you were me, how would you feel?"

Lynn puts her hands over her face and takes a deep breath. She again wipes the tears from her eyes and could not control her emotions. "Josh, I didn't want to ruin our wedding. I swear to you I was going to tell you tonight."

I respond to her. "Lynn, the decision has already been made. The die has been cast. You and your precious Board members chose to put this project on hold indefinitely. Then, you decide to lay off 20% of our R&D staff because the Parkinson's drug is put on hold. You also knew you could make that decision without me. I am not a Board member, so I am not privy to that information. Is this not correct, Lynn?"

Lynn looks at me and lets me know in no uncertain terms that we could be going around this topic all night and nothing will make her change her mind on the decision. She convinced me that she was being truthful and honest with me. So, she told me exactly what happened.

The Board of Directors met in an emergency meeting on Saturday, May 21st, when we were getting ready for our wedding. They called Lynn up, and they told her what they decided to vote on and why they decided to vote on the drug that was to be put on hold. Lynn explained that the data that went into the drug to get it passed through the FDA as quickly as possible, to satisfy Dr. Fringe and her fellow criminal Board members, then working for Medical Solutions, Inc., the predecessor to Differencia, was completely fabricated and falsified. If this information ever got out, we would never have a chance to get the right drug on the market. Once again, if not corrected now, criminal charges would probably be filed against our new company, Differencia, and we would be shut down.

Lynn explained to me that once the Parkinson's project was put on hold, there would be no need to employ the additional 20% of our research and development employees that we hired, or those that transferred from other departments, specifically for the Parkinson's project. We all agreed that everyone laid off from the Parkinson's project would be entitled to fifteen weeks of severance pay and outplacement services. They would be paid full medical benefits while receiving their severance pay. They would also be entitled to unemployment insurance and be the first on the list to be called back to work, when the Parkinson's project data would be correctly completed.

Finally, Lynn explained to me that she voted to put the project on hold under the circumstances, and so did Dr. Mulcahy. Once all the testing for the drug is completed by an independent research firm, which could be anywhere from three to six months down the road, we will resume our project. Lynn and I got up from the loveseat we had occupied for the past three hours getting through this ordeal, and went to bed in peace. Tomorrow is another day. Friday, I meet with the Board.

Chapter 14

Lessons Learned

Josh returns to the office and reviews the agenda items for the next Board meeting.

There are twenty-two items on the agenda.

Josh reflects that animosity ruins companies and that relationships between individuals are important.

Josh notices that he is scheduled to meet with the Human Resources Department. He is very confused about the reason for the meeting.

Interviews begin for the Director of Operations position. Josh meets with Mikayla, an MBA in Finance. She tells Josh that although she has done financially well in her current position, she wants to do more to promote the common good.

Mikayla divulges that Mr. Jones' 4-year-old daughter has Type 1 Diabetes and that he has Parkinson's disease. She relates that Mr. Jones has secured a patent on a revolutionary sailboat design, and as a result has become quite wealthy.

Mr. Jones receives a gloomy prognosis from his doctors, that he only has a few more years to live. He sells his business to spend more time with his family.

Mikayla reiterates her goal that promoting the common good is more important to her than to accumulate wealth. She wishes to make insulin more affordable to those suffering from Type 1 Diabetes and she wants to emphasize that she wants the Parkinson's drug to be approved by the FDA.

Josh walks down to the office of Reese Miles, Differencia's Human Resource Director.

Reese tells Josh that the Board his decided to downsize 20% of the Research and Development Department staff.

Josh responds very emotionally to the news. Reese expresses her surprise that Josh was not apprised of the news before the items were placed on the Board of Directors meeting agenda. Josh becomes indignant and says he will not make any decision on staff cuts until he meets with the Board, Lynn, Brody Young, and Dr. Mulcahy. He ponders the motivation for the staff cuts.

After working through the remainder of the agenda items, Josh goes home to discuss with Lynn the proposed staff cuts.

Josh asks Lynn if she knew of the proposed staff cuts. Lynn tells him that although she knew of them, she did not tell him so as not to spoil their wedding.

Josh feels betrayed by Lynn and accused her of betraying Differencia's core values.

Lynn indicates that her secrecy was not intended to deceive Josh and damage their relationship. She attests that her goal is to balance, as carefully as possible, her personal and professional lives.

Lynn asserts that she has a fiduciary responsibility to protect the interests of Differencia's investors and stakeholders. She refuses to reconsider her decision.

Once the Board's decision to provide the Parkinson's drug to the market was put on hold, there was no further need to retain 20% of the Research and Development Department personnel.

Lynn explains that once all the tests for the drug are completed, the project could be resumed and the laid off employees could be rehired.

Questions to Ponder

Should Lynn have withheld from Josh her knowledge that the Board had decided to cut 20% of the Research and Development Department staff? Why or why not? Have you ever been faced with a similar circumstance in your career?

To what extent should fiduciary responsibility dictate transparency between upper management and other Company employees?

To what extent do Companies have a responsibility to Company employees, when making decisions which affect employee compensation and livelihood? Do you struggle with this question in your Company?

What is your assessment of Josh's capabilities to be an effective CEO? Is his skill set sufficient to make him an effective leader? If so explain. If not, what skills does he need to develop to become a truly effective leader?

Do you consider Mikayla's decision to leave her current position and join Differencia a good one? Would this be damaging to her career?

Does Mikayla exhibit empathy for Mr. Jones' plight? What implications does this have for her desire to obtain an optimal balance between her professional and personal lives?

Do you think that Josh has an inferiority complex? If so, what is its origin? As his mentor, is Lynn an enabler in Josh's feelings of insecurity?

Josh's mental state is one of constant uncertainty. How should he address this? This can be effectively addressed by developing several scenarios and developing responses to these scenarios.

How solid is the personal relationship between Josh and Lynn? More trust and transparency are needed. How can these key leadership qualities be increased?

Is the Board of Directors' decision to put on hold, then to rehire the laid off staff after a decision is made, a justifiable one, or should the staff be retained in the hope of obtaining FDA approval?

Chapter 15
The Mulcahy Experience

It is Thursday, May 26th, 2022, and I am meeting at 9:00 A.M. with Dr. Mulcahy. She was summoned out of town to attend a conference at M.I.T. in Cambridge, MA, to get important updates on some of the formulas we use for drugs we manufacture. The conference lasted for three days, May 23rd, 24th, and 25th. Unfortunately, this leaves me only one day before the Board meeting, to sit down and talk to her about the Parkinson's drug release put on hold. We will also discuss the twenty percent reduction in our research and development staff ,which will affect fifty employees. These employees were pathologists, research scientists, oncologists, and neurologists. They are all highly paid employees with excellent benefits packages.

Lynn and I have been professional with each other, especially in the last few days, but cordial, especially in front of Jessica. I believe that Jessica is a speedy study, and it doesn't take her long to catch the friction between Lynn and me. Although I have accepted Lynn's explanation for keeping the Parkinson's project secret and the layoff secret, I am still struggling with her loyalty and trust in me. I can only assume right now that my readers, absorbing this transcript, believe that I am out of touch with my feelings and disconnected from the harsh realities handed to us in the corporate world. You may be right about me. Or you may be looking into your relationships and thinking it is not you that's disconnected, but rather your significant other not understanding you, and maybe for a good reason. BREAK

Someone told me a long time ago, and it always stuck in my head, that leadership is relational and not transactional. This keeps going through my head repeatedly. I don't know why or what it even means. I know that I am one confused and disoriented individual, in a sea of corporate monsters who are only out for their gain. I see what is happening here. The "greed" culture continues, and those who need to stand up to do the right thing are afraid to do the right thing and risk their corporate butts in the process. Isn't this the way companies are? Is this what we are too scared to admit? I now have problems dealing with me, let alone deception, with people I work with within the upper circles, including my wife and soulmate!

I am now at work, and it is 8:45 AM, approximately 15 minutes before I meet with Dr. Mulcahy to go over the agenda for Friday. The first item on our plan will be the Parkinson's drug project and the layoffs, among twenty other items dealing with the economic and financial states of Differencia.

It is 8:55 AM, and I'm sitting outside Dr. Mulcahy's office door. She waits until exactly 9:00 AM to open her door and welcome me in. She asked me if I had eaten breakfast, and I acknowledged that I did. She then asked me if I would like some water, and I said that it would be great with some ice and a slice of lime. She smiles, acknowledges my request, gets my water, and then sits down at the conference table, motioning me to join her.

Dr. Mulcahy and I open our notepads and turn on our personal computers to begin taking dubious notes at our meeting today. The mood in the office is quite somber, even melancholy. After about two minutes of staring at her computer, Dr. Mulcahy shouts at me. "Josh, what is your problem? Frankly, the expression on your face makes me very uncomfortable to be sitting here with you. I am picking up some very negative vibes. Anything going on between you and Lynn? Are you okay? Is Jessica, okay? And, most importantly, is Lynn, okay?"

I suddenly feel the adrenaline rushing through my body, as it did on Monday evening when Lynn broke the news about the Parkinson's project and the twenty percent staff layoff. My response to Dr. Mulcahy is as follows. "Bonnie, I have a fiduciary responsibility to the people that report to me, and you are one of them. My business partner, wife, or whatever you want to call her, did not tell me she was arranging with you to indefinitely postpone the Parkinson's project she and I had worked on for almost two years. The decision was made to lay off twenty percent of my R&D staff without my knowledge. How am I supposed to feel, Bonnie? I am Co-CEO of this Company, and I am responsible for making sure that I am kept in the loop on all decisions!"

Dr. Mulcahy takes a deep breath, sips a glass of ice water, and stares at me with such contempt that I am motionless to respond to her until she speaks. "Josh, you still have not found a way to protect that fragile ego of yours. You are the CEO of this company right now, with similar footage as "whatever you want to call her" on making decisions.

Josh, you could fire me right now. However, I would still be the Chair of the Board of Directors. You see, Josh, I don't have to be an employee of this Company or any Company to do what is right. I have just been insubordinate with you, Josh, and you have every right to reprimand me, give me a written warning, or maybe even show me the door." I continue to look at her without saying a word.

"The real thing is this, Josh: you want every protocol to be in your wheelhouse. You feel abandoned and deceived when you don't know what is always going on. You don't trust your people to make decisions independently, without your knowledge. Ultimately, your Co-CEO counterpart decided on something that you were unaware of, and you felt abandoned, deceived, and betrayed."

I respond to Dr. Mulcahy in kind. "Bonnie, is that what you are thinking about me right now?" She immediately responds, "Josh, you just don't get it, do you? I am not thinking about you right now. I am thinking about this Company. I am thinking about our agenda for tomorrow. You have just wasted fifteen minutes of my time talking about yourself and how deceived you were on Monday evening, in the privacy of your home with your wife and business partner. I don't have the luxury of time, pondering discussions with you and your wife."

I begin stuttering, and I don't know what to say in response. Her face is very red, and I could feel and sense the anger in her voice and body language. She continues. "Josh, on a matrix, I technically report to you as my CEO. However, we both report to the Board of Directors, of which I am a part. Lynn was prepared to tell you about our decision as Board members. Although you are the CEO, you could not participate in that decision. Josh, we did what was best for the Company, including you. You have no resources to run this Company, without the Board's blessing. Don't you get that?"

Finally, Dr. Mulcahy postures herself, takes a deep breath and grabs my hands. "Josh, you, me, and Lynn have worked hard on this Parkinson's project. I don't blame you for your feelings. Business decisions are often tough. I have decided as a Board member to lay off twenty percent of my staff. I don't know if I will ever get them back. They are all good people and precious scientists and doctors. No one wins in a layoff, Josh. It is an unfortunate, but often necessary decision to keep overhead expenses as low as possible, and reinvest in the Company to build it and make it stronger, making it attractive to investors. You should know that Josh. You are the finance guru, correct?"

I look up at Bonnie, and I say to her, "Why do I feel so deceived, not knowing about this?" She responds, "In business, Josh, sometimes to remain competitive, to survive, you have to 'March into hell for a heavenly cause.'" I suddenly remember in my economics class, when we studied utilitarian theory, it would help if you did things for the good of the many, and sometimes the few will take the brunt for the many. It is unintentional but occasionally necessary.

Finally, Dr. Mulcahy said something that made me think about how I've been acting the last few days. "Josh, Lynn has been parentless since she was just barely out of school. She and her sister Mary had to make it on their own. You were orphaned at a very young age, and you, too, had to make it on your own. You both did very well. You knew hard times more than most people. Your instinct is to survive. However, you can't confuse those instincts with remorse, demanding validation from the people you love the most. Don't do this until you know the whole story."

Somehow, I just learned one of the most valuable lessons. I realized I was not attacking Lynn consciously. Instead, I was shunning those that I love the most that couldn't love me back the way I wanted them to. They were my biological parents. I made this a smokescreen to not trust anyone or have anyone get too close to me, because I was afraid of getting hurt again. If I don't get over this, I can never become the best version of myself. I can never become the authentic leader I want to be. I owe Lynn an apology. I think I will bring her some flowers tonight and reflect on the lessons learned from today's session with Dr. Mulcahy.

Tomorrow is the big Board meeting. The Parkinson's project will be on the top with the layoffs and my vision going forward with this Company. Wish me luck!

Chapter 15 Lessons Learned

Josh meets with Dr. Mulcahy to discuss the Parkinson's drug release and the staff cuts scheduled in the Research and Development department.

Again, Josh questions trust and loyalty to him. He appears to be confused and disoriented.

Josh believes that a "greed" culture exists, in which companies put their pecuniary interests ahead of promoting the common good.

Dr, Mulcahy meets with Josh to review the agenda items for the Board meeting. She asks Josh why he appears to be very nervous.

Josh tells Dr. Mulcahy that it was wrong for her to keep secret from him, the delay in the release date for the Parkinson's drug and the layoff of the Research and Development department employees.

Dr. Mulcahy criticizes Josh for not being decisive in his dealings with her and Lynn. She asserts that if he deems their actions blameworthy, he has the prerogative to reprimand them.

Dr. Mulcahy states that Josh does not trust his people to make decisions independently, and that to be an effective leader, he must believe that she and Lynn have the best interests of Differencia at heart.

According to Dr. Mulcahy Josh's indecisiveness is driven by remorse, not objective thinking. He decides to apologize to Lynn.

Questions to Ponder

Is Dr. Mulcahy emerging as a mentor to Josh? If so, is she a good mentor?

In your past, have you ever been mentored by someone similar to Dr. Mulcahy? If so, how were you mentored? Was the effect on you positive or negative?

Do you agree with Josh that a "greed" culture exists today? Are individuals and companies subsumed with their own gain, as opposed to the goal of promoting the common good? Is it possible to achieve both goals simultaneously?

Is Josh justified in his reaction to Dr. Mulcahy's and Lynn's decisions to delay the Parkinson's drug release and to layoff the Research and Development department employees? Would you have handled the situation differently? If so, how would you have handled it?

Josh appears to be reluctant to allow his employees to act independently. Does this reflect a lack of trust? If so, how should he increase his trust in his employees? Do you have the trust of your employees? If not, how can you develop that trust?

In general, do you believe that employees have the best interests of their Company at heart, or are they primarily concerned with their own self interests? What is the culture in your Company?

Key Leadership Qualities Identified

Mentor - Authentic leaders serve as mentors, to assist others in becoming the best versions of themselves. A mentor gives constructive advice to others and is always focused on assisting others to accomplish their goals.

Rejection of the Greed Culture - Being concerned with both promotion of individual and corporate self interest, and concern for the common good. Authentic leaders are effective in achieving both goals simultaneously.

Sustainability - The ability to persist over time. Effective leaders are successful in maintaining their Company's culture over time. This requires both achievement of company financial goals and fulfilling the responsibility to preserve the existence of the entire world.

Reflection Period - Have you ever received disappointing news? It is imperative to process negative news and reflect on it before responding. This will lead to objective, rather than emotion-driven decision-making. How can you improve your powers of reflection?

Participative Decision-Making - Allowing others to assist you in making decisions. This will lead to different perspectives on an issue, which often results in creative solutions to complex problems. It is grounded in humility and the belief that others can help us to improve our decision-making.

Altruism - Unselfish regard for or devotion to the welfare of others. True leaders place the interests of the universe ahead of their own self interests. They realize that for the planet to continue to exist, it is necessary to promote the interests of all of humanity.

Chapter 16
The Board Meeting, Friday, May 27th, 9:00 AM

It is 4:30 AM by my digital alarm, and I can't fall back to sleep. This past week, while Lynn and I were celebrating our wedding, many decisions were made domestically and globally by so-called leaders, who promoted righteousness as the vital ingredient of their success. We now live in an environment of opinion polls driving our economy and sustainability into oblivious disorientation and misalignment.

Many of our leaders, including the high-powered influential ones, base their sense of accountability on those that accept their decisions as absolute and indisputable to anyone or anything. Subordinates are subsequently rewarded by their leaders with financial stability and increased power. In return, all these leaders ask from us is undivided loyalty and a promise of sustained protection in their inner circles.

Over the past twenty-five years, I have learned so much that makes me feel unsustainable in this so-called "corporate jungle" of capitalism, that builds a metamorphosis of deceit within an honest person's soul. This is what I wrestle with every day. Many of my colleagues may think of me as a mean-spirited parasite of corporate energy, having no direction or purpose in life. I can tell you unequivocally this is untrue. I would bet my bottom dollar that many of you reading this transcript in the present time would deny my feelings. Would you? Think again!

What would you do if you walked into this Board meeting that I am about to enter? What questions would you ask the Board? What type of questions would they be asking of you? You think you know all the answers, don't you? I want to stay in my comfort zone. I don't want to even think of the potential outcome, that I could be losing my wife to dementia because of the stress from this darn job! As you may be thinking, I don't see myself as a victim here. We are all supporters of corporate greed in one form or another, and I am an example of it.

I toss and turn all night and need to be bright, alert and ready for this Board meeting. I rise at 6:30 AM and decide to make myself some breakfast. Lynn and Jessica are both sleeping. I don't disturb them, despite the turmoil I am going through in my head. I will make myself scrambled eggs and dry wheat toast, and wash it down with a good strong cup of coffee. This should sustain me during our morning meeting, at least through break time. Dr. Mulcahy always allows us a break, after getting through the initial amenities and proceedings, including reading the minutes from the last meeting.

While I am making my eggs, I hear someone entering the bathroom on the first floor. Jessica is on the first floor. I check her bedroom, and she is still sleeping. She doesn't have to get up for school for another half hour, and then she does her routine with Lynn, as she does every day during the week. I call out to Lynn, and she responds affirmatively that she is the one in the bathroom. I ask her if she wants me to make her some breakfast, and she says she will have a glass of juice and have breakfast later with Jessica. I finish making my eggs, walk over to the refrigerator, and get Lynn a glass of juice and place it on the kitchen counter.

Lynn finishes up in the bathroom, and then proceeds to the kitchen and sits on one of the island counter stools. Her eyes are bloodshot, and she has an apprehensive look on her face. "Josh, I don't know how to say this, but I think you need me there at this Board meeting. I can help you get through this Board inquisition. I know how brutal these meetings can be sometimes. I have sat through many of them as CEO and a Board member."

I respond with kindness and gentleness. "Lynn, the last thing I would want to do is jeopardize your health. I only dread what it would be like for you to be incapacitated and not know me or your daughter. The outcome, due to stress, would be much more devastating than a Board meeting. I think that I can handle this. I've learned a lot from you and from the many people I have worked with. I think it is time for me to take my place and prove that I can do the right thing. I don't think you have to come this morning."

I could see Lynn's eyes getting a little bit misty. She reaches over to me and grabs my hands on the island counter. I can feel the energy between us, making me feel strong emotions that we are connected, whether we are separated physically or joined at the hip. "You are very kind, Josh, and very trusting. There isn't a person on the planet that I would want in that Board meeting this morning other than you.

I trust that you can handle the questions from the Board. However, many of them are still aware and apprehensive that you didn't call anyone to tell them what was going on when I was missing, and you were acting CEO in my absence." I remain silent and continue to look into Lynn's eyes ,so that she could continue her statement. "Human nature is that people don't forget easily about things. I think they are afraid that you will relinquish your responsibility once again with our newly formed company."

"Lynn, I will not disagree with you on this one. I admit that I relinquished my acting CEO responsibilities when you were missing. However, I am also human, and my humanity took over under the circumstances. I was overwhelmed with grief, fear, and a physical inability to function because of the sudden traumatic experience."

"Josh, people don't think about that. I know, and you know, that you were doing the best that you could do handling the situation, within the scope and limitations of the circumstances lying before you. As harsh as it might seem, people don't think that way. They only know that you didn't come through in a crisis and abandoned 11,000 employees who needed direction when I was missing.

"Josh, I am not the one who is judging you. However, the individuals judging you will decide on the resources we need to make Differencia go forward. What are you willing to sacrifice to make that happen?"

"Lynn, I must stop being the victim and truly convince myself that I am a leader. I must go into this Board meeting to prove that I am not acting alone and conferring with you on all decisions. We are a team. Do you think this is a good path?"

"Josh, my question to you is echoing back. Do you think this is a good path? It is not up to me anymore. We are Co-CEOs of Differencia. It is our choice to decide whether this is a good strategy. What say you?" I nod my head affirmatively. I get ready for my 9:00 AM meeting after consuming my breakfast, and Lynn goes in to wake up Jessica, have breakfast with her, and then bring her to school.

It is 8:15 AM. I have a 15-minute drive to work from my townhouse. I kiss my wife and daughter goodbye and head out to my big meeting with the Board of Directors. It is a beautiful day, and I feel very positive about meeting with the Board alone, after talking it over. I turn on the radio to get a little more relaxed before my meeting. However, I cannot get it out of my head, what Lynn said to me about the Board having trust in my ability to run this Company without her presence.

Something else I said to Lynn earlier this morning is bothering me. It is not about what she said to me, per se; it is more about what I said to her during a specific part of our conversation at the kitchen counter. "I must stop being the victim and truly convince myself that I am a leader. I must go into this Board meeting proving that I am not acting alone and conferring with you on all decisions. We are a team. Do you think this is a good path?"

It is good that I said I've got to stop being the victim. However, after thinking this through, I don't think it was very optimistic that I needed to convince myself that I am a leader, that I am not acting alone, and I confer with her on all decisions. This is such a contradiction. I can't have it both ways. If I don't think that I am a leader, and then convince the Board that I am not acting alone, what are they to think about my abilities if something should happen to Lynn and I was solely in charge of Differencia?

I must be honest with myself and admit that I am good at making speeches to defend myself. However, I never make speeches about protecting my team. If Lynn and I can't be a team, we can't work effectively to make this new enterprise work. If She is nonexistent because of potential illness in the future, why should the Board have confidence in me to drive this Company on and bring it to the next level of excellence?

Do I go into the Board meeting and act like Lynn does not exist in the decision-making process, trying to convince the Board that I can do this independently? Would they have confidence in me, since I have messed up so many times, especially during the crisis where I should've been accountable to my staff? Do I use my humanity to back up my rationale for not doing my job? Would they be forgiving without Lynn's input? Is she right about what they would think of me flying solo, with competitive sharks all around me, trying to take credit for a drug we developed, but is now put on hold because of a potential scandal? Once again, we put a product on the market that isn't ready.

How do I justify why this product was put on hold? Lynn and I have been going over this time and time again for the past two weeks, to prepare for this Board meeting today. We had gone over this with Dr. Mulcahy several times. It is now showtime, and I just arrived at work!

It is 8:55 AM, and Dr. Mulcahy greets me and walks me into the Boardroom. All Board members are present and accounted for. They greet us with a huge smile, and we are seated in our respective positions, the same seating as our last Board meeting. Just as in every other one, the minutes are read from the previous meeting and unanimously approved by the Board. I am ready for an all-day session. Dr. Mulcahy bangs her gavel, and the meeting commences.

The opening remarks at the Board meeting included a congratulatory note on my wedding with Lynn, which included best wishes and a long and sustainable happy life. Now, we are off to the races with the first agenda item. This will include questions from the Board members to me about Differencia's vision and mission statement, in reiteration of what we discussed in our last Board meeting before our wedding. It was a continuance of questions in priorities, to get the Parkinson's drug on the market as soon as possible. Then, the Board decided over the weekend of our wedding, in an emergency session, to put the Parkinson's drug on hold and cut twenty percent of our research and development staff. Dr. Mulcahy heads this operation until the drug is ready to be cleared by the FDA.

This could take three months, six months, or one year. The market is ready for the drug, and we are not. These are some of the questions I am about to face from the Board.

The first question comes from Dr. Brent Furan, a Board-certified neuropsychologist, who specializes in diseases of the mind, which include Alzheimer's and post-traumatic disorders.

His tone is very subtle and quite polished, as a highly educated individual with almost a cynical flair in his attitude toward me. This could be my imagination, because I know the question will have something to do with Lynn. She is not here to defend herself, and I must be cool, calm, and collected as CEO. His question follows. "Mr. Keating, what is the prognosis of Dr. Lynn Ann Marconi at present, to return to work in her full capacity within the next six months?"

I take a deep breath, and I posture myself to answer the question as a CEO and not as a defense weapon for Lynn. "Dr. Furan, I am not at liberty to discuss my wife's medical prognosis. You would have to obtain that information from her, with her permission. If I were to give you this information, I would be violating HIPAA laws, which is a federal violation. I believe you know that process."

Dr. Furan responds. "Mr. Keating, I am aware of the process, and I was not asking you the question referring to Dr. Marconi as your wife. I asked the question about her, like yourself, as an employee of Differencia. My intent was not to ask you about any medical records contained herein. It was simply her ability, having the highest position in this organization, to run the Company and make decisions that would influence 11,000 staff members."

I feel my blood boil, and I try very hard to control myself under the circumstances. However, I am only talking to the first Board member, and the meeting has just begun. Dr. Mulcahy chimes in. "Dr. Furan, please get to the point and tell me where this is going. If you want to ask a question about Dr. Marconi, and know she is not here to answer that question, please rephrase it as we have a long agenda ahead of us."

Dr. Furan rephrases. "Mr. Keating, assuming that there is a possibility that Dr. Marconi's prognosis is not favorable, after six months going forward, do you think you would be able to run this Company as CEO?"

I pause for a minute, fold my hands, and looked directly at him. "Dr. Furan, I do not have a crystal ball to predict the future. I intend to answer your question and all the Board members' questions, to focus on keeping this Company on track as a major competitor in a very competitive market.

Dr. Furan listens as I continue. "I have learned a lot over the past 25 years. I have had some wonderful mentors and not-so-wonderful mentors. I have experienced trauma, personal loss, and even depression. Each time I was able to get back on my feet, wipe myself off, and keep going. I may not have the rich background that many of the esteemed members of this Board possess. However, I know the ropes about this culture, this business, and most importantly, the core values that keep this Company solvent and competitive each day. If you want to ask me questions, ask me about that, and I will be glad to answer them."

It is break time, and Dr. Mulcahy bangs her gavel. We will continue our meeting with more questions from other Board members right after the break.

During the break, I am ready for another lecture about my performance in the Boardroom from Dr. Mulcahy. Instead, she looks over at me, smiles, and then gets some refreshments. I follow her to the refreshments to get coffee and a danish. Dr. Mulcahy smiles at me once again and walks away from the refreshment stand, over to a private area to sit down and enjoy her snack. My first impulse is to follow her to her quiet area and ask how I did. However, I stop myself, hold my confidence in my performance, and reflect on my efficacy.

I am a CEO, and technically, Dr. Mulcahy reports to me. Why would I be approaching her to validate my performance? Why would I want or need to get approval from her? For the first time in my life, I need to stand my ground as a leader. In fact, how can others lead in this Company if I don't show them that I can lead? I believe that Lynn did not see this in me this morning. Therefore, she offered to go with me to the Board meeting. She wanted to validate my performance as legitimate. She would only be validating her performance, which would de-legitimatize my ability to run the Company, should she become incapacitated. It is my turn to go back into the Boardroom and take on the questions from the next Board member. I remember saying to her this morning, "Lynn, I must stop being the victim and truly convince myself that I am a leader. I must go into this Board meeting to prove that I am not acting alone and conferring with you on all decisions. We are a team. Do you think this is a good path?"

After the break, we walk back into the Board meeting and greet the next Board member to ask me questions. Dr. Marcia Gibson is a general practitioner in the Los Angeles area. Her father was a philanthropist and a building developer in the Los Angeles area. Her family has donated millions to the LA Medical Center over the past several years. Her father was a research scientist in cardiac replacements, for those chronically ill with heart diseases. He was a well-known and respected surgeon in Los Angeles.

Dr. Gibson is middle-aged, very astute, and poised in appearance. She seems to handle herself in these situations quite well. She asks her first question in a very soft-spoken, melodious tone. "Mr. Keating, my family has dedicated their lives and money to science over the last two decades. My father, Dr. Raymond Gibson, became a cardiologist and a research scientist to save people's lives. Many individuals who invest in the greater good, believe that they can make a difference, in which they would leave the world a better place than it was before they entered it."

I don't know where Dr. Gibson is going with this, and frankly, I'm looking for some type of question in her monologue, which includes the historical background of her family. She continues. "Mr. Keating, my family has invested $3 million in developing the new Parkinson's drug. I want to know why, under your watch, this project was killed, and who decided to kill it!"

I am shocked, and can't believe what I heard from her. This is making absolutely no sense to me at all. Dr. Gibson is a Board member; I would think that she would have been one of the votes, by unanimous consent of the Board, to put the project on hold. I guess my assumption was wrong. This would mean that the Board, by a majority vote, decided to place the project on hold, and subsequently laid twenty percent of the research and development staff. Dr. Mulcahy is a part of that staff, and the head of the R&D department. My first impulse is to look at Dr. Mulcahy and study the expression on her face, while Dr. Gibson asks me why this project has been placed on hold. I am the CEO of this Company, and I am clueless about how to answer her.

I respond to her. "Dr. Gibson, with all due respect, it was not my decision to put this project on hold. The Board had voted in an emergency meeting last week, when I was preparing for my wedding, to put this project on hold. Since I report to the Board and am not a part of the Board, this vote was taken in secrecy. I am assuming that you had a paper vote, rather than a headcount, because of the nature and sensitivity of this decision. Is that not correct?"

The silence in the Boardroom is deafening, after Dr. Gibson's question. She responds to me in the affirmative. "Josh, I only knew the outcome of the tally and who cast the deciding vote. The vote was five in the affirmative and five in the negative. As the Board Chair, Dr. Mulcahy broke the tie with an affirmative vote. The vote was narrowly margined in the affirmative, six for and five against."

My mind is racing, because I honestly do not know how to answer the question. I am oblivious to how or why the Board voted the way they did, but I am also undeniably out of the loop as the new CEO on how to answer this Board member. As CEO, it is my responsibility to defend this organization's core values, which call for total transparency. In reality, ex parte of a business relationship with Lynn, my wife, I am on a whole new playing field. I am a sailor in a boat without a paddle.

Dr. Gibson continues as the tears begin flowing down her cheeks. "Josh, I lost my father to Parkinson's disease. On his deathbed, he made me promise to see this project through, and to donate the $3 million to save others who are going through this horrible disease. I now am speaking with half of the CEO team, who knows nothing about why the project was put on hold and voted to put it on hold by majority consent, including the Board Chair, Dr. Mulcahy."

There's an expression that it is very lonely when you are at the organization's top. Now I can see why that expression is so true. This conversation with Dr. Gibson is very painful for me. However, it is equally, if not more painful, for Dr. Gibson. If I am to be an authentic leader, I must be able to deal with the truth and promote total transparency.

Until this morning, I had no idea how the vote turned out by this Board of Directors, which put the Parkinson's project on hold, costing the jobs of 50 individuals and affecting their families and their livelihoods for an indefinite period.

Leadership has to do with making effective business decisions, which are sometimes very painful. We are often told that utilitarian theory is a business model for finding solutions to problems that benefit the good of the many. However, many good people lose out, resulting in what our economists call "redundancies." Individuals inadvertently become servitude of their destinies, without justification or rationale of purpose. It is a misnomer to think that rational business decision-making will always be correct and without risk.

Leaders need to take risks, or they can't compete. Putting this Parkinson's drug on hold was not an easy decision. The thing that bothers me is that it had been put on hold because of bad business decisions, made by corrupt members of the Board of Directors, that were associated with then Medical Solutions, Inc. However, these Board members are no longer with this organization. Differencia inherited the original sin of Medical Solutions; Inc. Dr. Gibson was one of the replacements of the corrupt Board members. The latter was asked to leave after the scandal was discovered. Dr. Gibson came on Board when Differencia was formed.

Not knowing about the scandal, Dr. Gibson invested her family's money in the new organization. I lived through the scandal with my then business partner and now wife, Dr. Lynn Ann Marconi. She almost lost her life because of corruption in the upper circles of then, Medical Solutions, Inc. I have now been chosen by my wife, business partner, Board member, and, finally, Co- CEO of Differencia, to lead this organization.

Dr. Mulcahy asks for a brief recess and tells Dr. Gibson she would allow her time to continue her questioning after the break. During our break, Dr. Mulcahy pulls me aside in private and asked me if I think I should continue with Dr. Gibson, or table her questions to a different part of the day when I had time to think about my answers. I tell her I will let her know right after the break. She smiles, walks away from me, and gets some refreshments.

At the end of the break, Dr. Mulcahy asks me again about my preferences going forward with Dr. Gibson. I respond that I am ready to continue with her, once we commence our meeting. Dr. Mulcahy smiles at me, and we walk into the Boardroom. She sits down and bangs her gavel. Dr. Gibson is prompted to ask the next question.

"Mr. Keating, although you were not aware that the Parkinson's project was put on hold, I would assume that you would not have known what led to the Board decision, correct?" I am in a real bind. I don't know how to skirt around answering this question. I feel so alienated and alone. As CEO, I am responsible for the bottom line, and no one can take responsibility for this answer but me. I cannot blame anyone for pushing me into this position. I accepted the job and all the responsibilities that go along with it.

I can't point the finger at Lynn, who told me why the project was postponed. I can't blame Dr. Mulcahy, although she was the deciding vote to put the project on hold, knowing that the data was incomplete and would fail with the FDA. This would destroy any chances of the Parkinson's drug becoming a reality. It may even be the demise of Differencia, if the application was resubmitted without verification of proof of analysis after testing. It would take 3 to 6 months before the testing is completed.

Dr. Gibson waits for an answer, and the Board is silent. I clear my throat and proceed after taking a drink of water. "Dr. Gibson, as you know, I have been selected by my Co-CEO, Dr. Lynn Ann Marconi, to help plan and execute a vision and mission for our new company, Differencia. I have a long history standing with me on this company's predecessor, Medical Solutions, Inc. As you are aware, you have been selected, based on your medical history and your father's philanthropy, to serve as a member of its Board of Directors."

She listens intently as I continue. "There is no easy way to say this, Dr. Gibson. Differencia's reasons for wanting you to become a member of our Board and the rationale to have you join Differencia was your passion for obliterating Parkinson's disease and receiving your $3 million contribution to help fund the research to make that happen."

One of the other Board members chimes in, Dr. Craig Foster, a Board-certified pharmacist, and philanthropist. He was one of the founders of Medical Solutions, Inc. He has a long history with this entire organization and its culture.

He asks, "where is this going. Mr. Keating? We are on a very tight schedule today, with many items left to go, in which you must preside over." I address him immediately. "With all due respect, Dr. Foster, I will be done shortly, and I need your undivided attention, to listen to what I'm about to say because it affects all of you. What I'm about to say will affect this Board, the 11,000 staff members that we employ, and, finally, the thousands of people around the world who we give hope that they can rid themselves of their afflictions by the drugs that we make." He allows me to continue without interruption.

"Dr. Gibson, the truth of the matter is that in the transition from Medical Solutions, Inc. to Differencia, we inherited the sins of the previous company, which included the falsification of data that we believed was cleared, before we were to resend it to the FDA for final approval. Dr. Mulcahy, the head of the research team, discovered that Dr. Fringe, the Director of the Board of Directors of the prior company, Medical Solutions, Inc., did not rewrite the application to the FDA as "incomplete" within the application submission deadline dates. As a result, the application was put on hold to prevent further problems with the FDA."

Dr. Gibson responds. "So, you knew about this, Mr. Keating, and you didn't tell us anything about it before the vote." There are all types of scattered chatter shared among the Board members. At this point, Dr. Mulcahy decides to break for lunch, after she announces that this conversation will be continued with the Board members in the afternoon, as it is a top priority.

The Board breaks for lunch, which is about one hour, and I go to my car to call Lynn. I explained to her everything that went on in the morning conversations with Dr. Furan and Dr. Gibson. Dr. Mulcahy and Lynn go on a three-way strategic conference call, on what to do when questions resume by Dr. Gibson in the afternoon session. We all agree as a team that Lynn, as Co-CEO and voting Board member, should join our meeting by teleconference, as we resume the afternoon session.

After lunch, Lynn joins us on a video conference call. She speaks to Dr. Gibson. "Dr. Gibson, at present, I am of sound mind and body and share CEO responsibilities with my business partner, Josh Keating. I need to keep my stress levels down, as per the doctor's orders. However, in no way is my thinking affected by my illness at this time."

Dr. Gibson remains silent and allows Lynn to continue the video conference call. "Dr. Gibson, for the past year, Dr. Mulcahy, Josh, and I have been working on keeping this organization afloat, to the point of starting over with a new vision and new mission. We created Differencia. This would give everyone a chance to start fresh, keep all our employees, and introduce drugs to the market, including a new

Parkinson's drug, that could change many lives for the better, many years into the future."

Dr. Gibson is staring intently into the videoconference screen, as are the other Board members. Lynn continues. "Josh and I are of one mind and body when it comes to servicing this organization. We have vowed that we will have continued transparency and eliminate the past scandals. If we have any hope of getting this Parkinson's drug on the market, which is your dream, you need to work with us and give us the resources we need to make it happen. However, we must do it the right way. We can't cut corners, and we must be honest with each other."

Tears flow from Dr. Gibson's eyes. I observe the other Board members listening to Lynn with unabated attention. "Dr. Gibson, we want your dream to come true. Josh was very honest with you today, and he was transparent. He was aware that I was in his corner, but could not physically help him. He had to do this independently and prove he was a leader. As CEO of two companies for several years, I cannot tell you how proud I am of him right now!" Dr. Mulcahy takes off her glasses and rubs her eyes as Lynn continues.

"We need the support of each Board member going forward. I can only promise you that Josh and I will continue to work relentlessly to do the right thing. Our efforts have been and will continue to be sincere. I ask you to do the same. Whatever the future brings, it's in our hands."

Chapter 16

Lessons Learned

Before the Board meeting, Josh reflects on the state of the economy and the role current day corporations play in influencing economic outcomes. He believes that corporate subordinates are rendered power and are given financial stability in return for their loyalty.

Josh muses that he is a victim of corporate greed and worries about the dementia that Lynn is experiencing because of job stress. He tries to anticipate the questions he will be asked in the Board meeting.

Lynn tells Josh she wants to attend the Board meeting to support him. Josh responds by saying he wants to attend the meeting without her, in order to reduce any stress on her.

Lynn states that she worries that the Board will question why Josh did not tell them why she was missing, when the Parkinson's drug announcement was to be made. She tells Josh that the Board may have serious concerns that he did not come through in a crisis, and abandoned 11,000 employees who needed direction in her absence.

Josh is indecisive on how to proceed. Should he attend the meeting without Lynn? Lynn tells Josh that it is his call. He continues to be plagued by indecision.

Josh wonders if the Board will have confidence in him without Lynn being present. How can he justify why the announcement of the Parkinson's drug was put on hold?

Dr. Mulcahy and Josh enter the Boardroom. She calls the meeting to order.

The first agenda item will include questions from Board members about Differencia's vision and mission statements. Josh must explain to the Board why the Parkinson's drug announcement was not made.

Dr. Brent Furan, a Board-certified neuropsychologist, asks Josh about the prognosis for Lynn to return to work at her full capacity within the next six months.

Josh tells Dr. Furan that because of HIPAA laws, he is unable to discuss Lynn's medical prognosis without her permission.

Dr. Furan responds by saying he's not asking for Lynn's medical records.

Dr. Mulcahy expresses irritation with Dr. Furan and asks him to rephrase his question.

Dr. Furan asks Josh if he would be able to run Differencia as CEO if Lynn was incapacitated.

Josh indicates that despite setbacks in his personal and professional life, he has been able to overcome these adversities and move on to meet future challenges.

Before returning to the Boardroom, Josh tells himself that he must convince the Board that he is confident and that he can lead Differencia as CEO in Lynn's absence.

After a break, Josh returns to the Boardroom and is questioned by Dr. Marsha Gibson, a general practitioner in the Los Angeles area. Doctor Gibson indicates that her family has dedicated their lives and money, over the past two decades, to Parkinson's drug research. She asserts that her family has invested $3 million in developing the new drug and she asks Josh why the project was killed and who killed it.

Josh responds by saying that it was not his decision to put the project on hold.

Dr. Gibson indicates that all she knew was that the vote was 6-5 in the affirmative with Dr. Mulcahy casting the deciding vote.

Dr. Gibson laments that on his deathbed, her father made her promise to see the project through, and donate $3 million to save others afflicted by Parkinson's.

Josh reflects that corrupt and self-serving corporate motives often distort ethical decision-making. The decision to put on hold the release of the Parkinson's drug ,was based on bad business decisions by corporate members of the Board of Medical Solutions.

Dr. Mulcahy calls for a brief recess and asks Josh if he wants to continue with Dr. Gibson's line of questions. He agrees to continue.

Dr. Gibson asks Josh if he knew what led to the decision to put on hold the Parkinson's drug announcement.

Josh is confused on how to answer. Who's at fault? Dr. Mulcahy? Lynn? Or himself?

Josh responds by saying that Dr. Gibson was approached to be a Board member, in order to obtain $3 million to fund Parkinson's drug research.

Dr. Craig Foster, a certified pharmacist, presses Josh to explain further his role in delaying the decision to make the Parkinson's drug announcement.

Josh states that the transition from Medical Solutions to Differencia was fraught with falsification of data, before it was sent to the FDA for final approval. The Board of Directors of Medical Solutions did not rewrite the application within the submission deadline, and as a result the application was put on hold to prevent further problems with the FDA.

Dr. Gibson reprimands Josh for not telling the Board about the falsification of data, which prevented the announcement from taking place.

After a lunch break, Dr. Mulcahy, Josh, and Lynn agree that Lynn, as Co-CEO, will join the meeting by teleconference.

Lynn reports to Dr. Gibson that she is healthy enough to share CEO responsibilities with Josh. She asserts that for the past year she, Dr. Mulcahy, and Josh, have formed a new organization called Differencia, with a new mission and vision statement.

Lynn asks the Board for the resources necessary to fulfill Differencia's mission and vision statements. She indicates that she has full confidence in Josh's ability to lead effectively.

Do you believe that corporations have given their employees power and financial stability in return for their loyalty?

Josh believes that his firing was the result of corporate greed. Do you agree with him? Why or why not?

Lynn tells Josh that she wants to attend the Board meeting to support him. Is this a good idea? Why or why not? Does this cut against her belief that he "can go it alone?"

Josh is uncertain as to whether he should attend the meeting alone. Does his uncertainty in decision making indicate that he is weak in being decisive?

Josh appears to have difficulty in concentrating on his thoughts. Do you think he has ADHD? If so, what can he do to focus more effectively? Do you show signs of ADHD? What can you do to increase your powers of concentration?

In response to Dr. Furan's question about Lynn's medical condition, does Josh give a satisfactory answer? Would you have answered differently?

Does Josh give a satisfactory answer to Dr. Gibson's question, as to why the Parkinson's project was put on hold? Explain your answer. How would you have handled the situation?

How would you evaluate Dr .Mulcahy's leadership effectiveness? Is her approach to securing Board support to delay applying for the FDA approval promising, or does it lack true transparency?

What is your assessment of Dr. Gibson's motives? Is her advocacy to get the Parkinson's drug approved driven by the financial resources her family has committed to the project a valid position to take? Why or why not? Explain your answer. If you were in her shoes, would you have acted differently?

Is the Board being too cautious in putting the project on hold, given that there would be significant layoffs within Differencia? Explain your answer. Would you have acted differently? Should the project be allowed to continue in the short run while research continues?

Effective leadership requires making decisions under circumstances of uncertainty. Should the Board have been more proactive in bringing the drug to market?

Key Leadership Qualities Identified

Empowerment - Authority or power given to someone to do something. The process of becoming stronger and more confident in controlling one's life and claiming one's rights. Empowered employees are highly likely to be very proactive in contributing to company gold achievement.

Delegation - Assigning a task or responsibility to another person, typically one who is less senior than oneself. This is based on trust and allows the delegated person to develop their skills. It leads to helping others become "the best version of themselves."

Political Acumen - Authentic leaders are aware of the surrounding social environment and provide guidance to their followers. A leader takes people where they want to go. A great leader takes people where they don't necessarily want to go, but ought to be.

Objectivity - Expressing or dealing with facts or conditions as perceived, without distortion by personal feelings, prejudices, or interpretations. Effective leaders are not influenced by the impact of their decision on their personal circumstances.

Likeability - Having pleasant or appealing qualities. Likeable individuals tend to attract others easily. This increases the chances that their views will be listened to, which allows leaders to promote their agenda.

Chapter 17

Lynn and Mary Marconi, Monday, June 6th, 11:23 AM

Happy Monday! I am ready to begin the week just like any other week. It's 7:30 AM. I kiss my wife and daughter goodbye. Only God knows when I'll be coming home tonight, or any other night. This is why I guess they put a couch in the CEO's office. Business never sleeps.

After getting a latte and a danish at Starbucks, I get to my office at 8:00 sharp. My assistant hands me my agenda items for the day, beginning at 8:30 AM. My schedule is jam-packed with appointments and meetings through 7:00 PM. This is a typical day for me. There are no significant interruptions or disruptions.

I am into my fourth meeting of the day, and about ready to go into my next meeting at 11:30 AM. I will be meeting with Board members Dr. Marcia Gibson, Dr. Ingrid Frost, and Mr. Jesse Finkelstein, a real estate developer. Mr. Finkelstein has helped build two wings dedicated to treating Alzheimer's disease and rehabilitation, at the Los Angeles Medical Center. One of the wings constructed by his Company was dedicated and named after his Dad, whom he lost to Alzheimer's in 1982.

I check my watch as I enter the meeting with the Board members. The time is 11:23 AM, and my cell phone is buzzing. The incoming call reads, "Lynn Marconi." I immediately pick up the call, and Lynn is sobbing. My first impulse before she says anything was that something happened to Jessica at school. "Lynn, what's wrong? Did something happen to Jessica?" "Josh, I just got a call from my sister Mary. She has been diagnosed with Parkinson's disease. It's in the early stages."

I am beside myself, and walking into a meeting with Board members to discuss the outcome of the last Board meeting, and the decision to put the Parkinson's drug project on hold pending further investigation. The decision to put the project on hold narrowly passed, by a six to five majority vote, and the Board Director was the tiebreaker. The decision was split as the tiebreaker vote was a technicality that could've gone either way.

Lynn cries out to me, "Josh, you have to convince the Board members to take the project off hold status and resume the research as quickly as possible." I respond, "Lynn, you need to calm down. I am sorry to hear about your sister Mary. However, she is not the only one diagnosed with Parkinson's today. Things do get somewhat sticky when they hit in our back yard. We will talk about this tonight when I get home."

There is a pause on the phone, and the dead air feels like an eternity. "Lynn, are you still there?" Still, there is no response. Finally, Lynn does respond, and I get a sense of relief, considering her condition. "Josh, I apologize for calling you up in such a panic. Mary is my twin sister, and I'm scared, Josh. I am scared." I pause a second or two. "I know you're scared, baby. We will get through this, like everything else. We always persevere. I'll see you tonight, and we will discuss the whole thing. We know there is always a solution if we think it through together."

Lynn responded favorably for the time being, and I asked her to give Jessica a big kiss for me after school. I said to tell her I love her and will see her tonight. I hung up the phone and began walking to my next meeting with the three Board members I mentioned earlier. It is difficult for me to walk into a meeting with Board members after getting the news I just received. However, this is part of my job. I can't let distractions get in the way of my focus and thought process during this meeting.

As I walk into the conference room, my cell phone buzzes again. The incoming text message is from Dr. Mulcahy. "Josh, please meet me in my office when you get a minute. I have some news to share and need to keep you in the loop." I immediately text her back. "I have a full schedule today. Can this wait?" She texted me back, "I'm afraid this is something you'll want to hear and discuss as soon as possible. Please give me any time you can to meet with me during the day. I'll make the time on my end, to make sure that happens." I text her back. "How about my fifteen-minute lunch break this afternoon, between 1:00 and 1:15 PM?" She texted back, "Fine, Josh, whatever you can give me." I respond, "Okay, see you then."

I finally arrive in the conference room. The three Board members are waiting for me, and we begin discussing the Parkinson's project.

Dr. Frost opens the discussion. "For the last decade, I have been researching Parkinson's, including thyroid diseases. I have consulted with several pharmaceutical companies on drug development, following all the guidelines to get approved by the FDA for the drug I helped develop. I sit on this Board of Directors to ensure that the work this Company puts into getting FDA approval is followed through to the letter. I am laser-focused on dotting every 'I' and crossing every 'T' on all data about the research I lead."

I continue to listen attentively to Dr. Frost. "Josh, we are not a charity. We are a business. Without us, many peoples' lives would end a lot quicker, had they not been using the drugs we developed and continue to develop." I feel this lump in my throat because I don't know where Dr. Frost is going at this point. However, I continue to hear her out.

"As Co-CEO of this company, you have a fiduciary obligation to assure that this business is profitable and achieves its goals and objectives. Without success in our research to get our drugs on the market, the opportunity cost would be to go out of business. Can you afford to do that? Can you afford to rob all the people that work in this Company of their salaries? Can you afford not to achieve the goals and objectives we strategically planned when we started this new Company, Differencia?"

I remain silent and keep listening. "Your job is to have our investors believe that our drug will work, based on sound scientific research.

I am not concerned with who voted and why they came to this Board's conclusions. Your job was not to let this problem go as far as it did. This Board should have unanimously voted to go forward with this project. Essentially, it was a split vote, and the Board Chair, Dr. Mulcahy, took a no-confidence vote in this project, based on her vendetta with Dr. Fringe." *Please read The Authentic Leader, authored by John DiCicco and Robert Cuomo, to learn more about Dr. Fringe.*

At this point, I don't know what to say. I just became a Co-CEO of this Company. I had no idea what was going on with the Board vote, and was kept out of the loop by Board Chair, Board member, Co-CEO, my wife and life partner, Dr. Lynn Ann Marconi. Is this all my fault? I am alone here and being snowballed by these Board members. I begin taking notes and keep silent. The best thing for me to do right now is to listen, take it all in, and take it all under advisement.

Mr. Jesse Finkelstein, a real estate developer, is speaking. "Mr. Keating, as you know, I lost my father to Alzheimer's in 1982. This was personal. I am a successful real estate developer, and have invested over $30 million from my Company in adding two entire hospital wings to the Los Angeles Medical Center, in memory of my Dad. However, I realized that while building these hospital wings, dedicated solely to the research and accommodation of Alzheimer's patients, I was accomplishing something I could never do alone. I needed talented people like you have in this company, to bring my goals and objectives to fruition. It may not be today. It may not be tomorrow, but it will happen."

I listen intently as Mr. Finkelstein continues. "You have a remarkable team in this Company of dedicated individuals, who have been providing incredible breakthroughs, through research, to help people stay alive longer and with a lot less pain from their diseases." He finally ends his conversation with me with the following statement. "Josh, whether you knew or didn't know how the vote went for this Parkinson's project, it should have no bearing on how you advocate to see it through to fruition. Stay focused on the goals, and I will give you my full support. This is a promise, Josh."

Mr. Finkelstein now yields the conversation to Dr. Marsha Gibson, as I continue to take notes. "Mr. Keating, it is nice to see you again. I want to focus on the $3 million my Dad donated to develop this Parkinson's drug. For the life of me, I still can't figure out why, as Co-CEO, you can justify keeping this project on hold. Do you have any answers, Mr. Keating?"

I stop taking notes, close my notepad and compose my thoughts carefully before responding. "Dr. Frost, Mr. Finkelstein, and Dr. Gibson. You have asked riveting questions and made significant comments in today's meeting. However, I am sure this will be the first of several meetings in the future, relating to the Parkinson's project. I will have to take all this under advisement and meet with my team before our next Board meeting, scheduled for June 23rd, which I believe is a Monday."

Mr. Finkelstein's response is quite direct and to the point. "Josh, as you know, I am not only a Board member, but also a major investor in this Company. My two colleagues sitting to the left and right of me are also investors. You need our resources to continue this project, giving us a return on our investment. I know you know this is the right thing to do. It is good for the people we serve and for the Company, to continue its mission and strategic plan. We will give you one week to come up with some answers on how you will continue this project. And, from what the 'ground patrol' tells us, it will take three to six months to send a completed application to the FDA for approval. This timeframe will not be acceptable. We want you to fix this problem, and soon."

I am pretty taken aback by Mr. Finkelstein's demand, and let him know in no uncertain terms that I will have to discuss this with my team. He immediately responds, and quite harshly. "Mr. Keating, you are telling me that it takes three to six months to fix the problem on an application that has already weathered the storm twice, starting with Dr. Fringe. She is no longer with the Company. Then, you made a second attempt to send it back to the FDA, after allegedly the problem was cleared. Finally, you put it on hold again, telling me it is not removed."

I could feel my blood boiling. I try to refrain from being contemptuous toward Mr. Finkelstein. I fold my hands, put my head down and lift it slowly, looking directly at him. "Mr. Finkelstein, I must do the right thing and not set this Company right back to square one with this

Parkinson's drug, if I am to be that lucky. Suppose it ever gets out that we sent in falsified information. In that case, we will not only lose the Parkinson's drug project, but we may be indicted on criminal charges of falsifying information."

Dr. Foster chimes in here, as a professional immunologist and renowned researcher. "Mr. Keating, you are not focusing on our concern. Rather, you are focused on an alibi to justify putting the drug on hold. Is this not true?" I respond quickly, "I disagree." Dr. Foster ignores my comment and continues with her point. "Mr. Keating, I couldn't care less about your justification for supporting the drug that has been put on hold for data that is incomplete. Focus on the facts, please! Rather, our concern is that we accurately submit the correct data in less time than the three to six months you quoted me to get it to the FDA. We have the technology to do that, and I can help. Are you aware that once the application is submitted to the FDA, they usually decide to approve it within ten months?

"However, there are many phases of drug testing, research, and experimentation, placebo tests, etc., preceding the drug approval process, that needs to be verified on the FDA application before it is submitted for FDA consideration. That process can take anywhere from ten to fifteen years. We started this research at Medical Solutions as employees many years ago. This is our 'Cadillac invention.'"

I am speechless at this point, and Dr. Gibson now begins to speak. "Josh, why would three Board members in this room donate millions of dollars of their family fortunes, for a drug we don't believe will work? We need to do it right, not put it on hold. We are almost there. You are the CEO. Lynn is the CEO. You both have accounting backgrounds. We can't lose investors because they lose faith in our efforts. I would rather lose all my money on something that fails rather than something we've abandoned. We need to make every effort for this drug to succeed or all our research will have been for nothing." I listen intently as Dr. Gibson continues. "You always talk to us about opportunity costs when it comes to cash flow. Think of what we would give up by wasting valuable time doing nothing to advance our project. In our field, six months is like an eternity."

I am looking at Dr. Gibson and clearly see her point. I can also understand why the vote from the Board to put this on hold was so divided. I clearly missed the point. Every day now, this project is on hold, without any pressure to get it through. It's another day of frustration for our investors, who believe this Company can make a difference. I now realize that two major investors have lost loved ones because they didn't have cures for the diseases that took their parents' lives. This gave them hope.

I promise the Board members that I would get them an answer by the end of the week. I tell them I will meet with Lynn and Dr. Mulcahy, and convince them to take another Board vote ASAP, even as early as the end of the week.

I am home at almost 8:00 PM. Jessica is fast asleep. Lynn is sitting on the love seat and in total shock and despair over her twin sister's diagnosis. I put down my briefcase, loosen my tie and sit next to her. She still managed to have dinner ready, and waited for me to eat. She had set a beautiful table for two, an aromatic candle between our dishes, casting a romantic shadow on us, and a sweet cinnamon scent throughout the house. Lynn puts her head on my lap and looks up as I wipe the tears from her bloodshot eyes.

Lynn says, "First me, Josh, now Mary. She is my twin, and I voted to put a drug on hold that would help her." Lynn pauses and waits for my reaction before she explains what happened when the vote was taken. My response was swift. "Lynn, you voted to detain the application process until we got the data, right? Then you and the Board agreed by a narrow margin to resubmit the application for approval, when the testing was properly completed in three to six months. Is this correct?" There is always a technicality in words when it comes to intent. Lynn responds, "Josh, the data was verified, and the results came in two weeks ago. An independent research agency conducted the tests. The drug is ready to be submitted for FDA approval."

At this point, I am completely thrown by this news. I tell Lynn I don't understand. She continues. "Mulcahy knew the drug was approved, and convinced me the data was still incomplete, to get me to vote to put it on hold."

I am entirely out of the loop and exhausted from the day. Maybe

I am not hearing this right. I ask Lynn again. "Why did Mulcahy withhold this information from you? Why is she playing both sides of the fence?" Lynn responds. "Fringe got a whiff that our drug might be getting approved by her sources (she had many) and was ready to blow the whistle on us for sending a falsified report to the FDA, saying she had the proof. Ultimately, she would give this information to our competition and file with the FDA to have us investigated." I tell Lynn that this is unbelievable. I ask her, "Who gave Mulcahy the 'heads up' to do the independent report after learning what Fringe was trying to pull?" Lynn responds, "One guess. Times up!" My response: "Jonathan Peters?" Lynn looks at me and smiles.

I finally figure out what happened. The Board was not aware of what Mulcahy knew about Dr. Fringe, and she kept the Board and me out of the loop on purpose. They take a five-to-five vote. Mulcahy is the tiebreaker. Jonathan tells his sources to ensure the information gets back to Fringe, that the project was put on hold. Fringe is in the clear to spread the news to our competition. When Dr. Fringe developed the Parkinson's drug, she was an employee of Medical Solutions, which no longer existed, and the drug was never correctly patented. It was only submitted for preliminary approval. Final approval was never verified after the scandal was discovered. The data was not correctly verified through testing, although Fringe lied and said it was.

Lynn says, "Josh, we are voting tomorrow to approve sending the drug to the FDA." I ask her, "Was this a setup by the Board members that visited me today?" Lynn just looks at me and smiles. "No, Josh, it was not. I had a conference call with Mulcahy this morning, just before I got the call about my sister, and she explained everything to me; how ironic! "I respond. "Then it is true about Mary?" Lynn says, "Yes, Josh. Let's get the drug on the market after we have dinner!"

Chapter 17
Lessons Learned

Josh arrives at his office and reviews the agenda for the morning Board meeting. He will be meeting with Board members Dr. Marsha Gibson, Dr Ingrid Frost, and Mr. Jesse Finkelstein, a real estate developer.

Lynn calls Josh to tell him that her sister Mary has been diagnosed with Parkinson's disease. She tells Josh that he needs to tell the Board that they must resume the project as soon as possible.

Josh tells Lynn that they can discuss the issue when he comes home that night.

Dr. Mulcahy calls Josh and requests a meeting with him as soon as possible.

Once the Board meeting begins, Josh is questioned by Dr. Frost. She tells him that she is focused on getting the Parkinson's drug approved in compliance with FDA standards.

Dr. Frost tells Josh that if the research does not continue, the Company will go out of business, and several thousand employees will lose their jobs. She criticizes him for not being proactive in going forward with the project.

Josh is questioned by Mr. Jesse Finkelstein, a real estate developer, who lost his father to Parkinson's disease. He indicates that he has donated over $30 million to Los Angeles Medical Center.

Mr. Finkelstein praises Josh and his team for the great work they have done in Parkinson's drug research. He tells Josh that he should weigh all perspectives in making the decision as to whether or not to go forward with the drug, and that he will support him regardless of his decision.

Dr. Gibson tells Josh that she cannot understand his decision to keep the project on hold, given that her father contributed to funding research on the drug's effectiveness.

Mr. Finkelstein explains that the Company must continue to go forward with its mission and strategic plan. He tells Josh that he has one week to get back to the Board, as to how he will continue with the project. He asserts that Josh has failed twice to bring the drug to the FDA for approval.

Josh responds that in good conscience he cannot send a request for approval to the FDA, based upon falsified information.

Dr. Foster instructs Josh to submit a fully developed and safe Parkinson's drug to the FDA for approval in less than three to six months. She asserts full FDA approval of the drug could take 10 to 15 years, given the many phases of drug testing, research, and experimentation. She contends that if the project does not go forward immediately, many investors will lose faith in the Company and the Company will be on the verge of insolvency.

Josh answers that he will provide a response to Board concerns within a week.

Upon returning home, Josh tells Lynn that he understands that new data indicates that the drug is now ready for approval. Lynn asserts that Dr. Mulcahy knew the drug was approved and told her to put the project on hold.

Lynn states that Dr. Mulcahy heard that the project would go forward, and that Dr. Fringe would accuse the Company of sending a falsified report to the FDA.

Jonathan Peters tipped off Dr. Mulcahy about Doctor Fringe's past actions, in lying about the drug's safety.

Lynn asserts that a vote will be taken tomorrow, to recommend sending the drug to the FDA for approval.

Questions to Ponder

When Lynn learns of Mary's Parkinson's diagnosis, is her recommendation to go ahead with the project justifiable? Why or why not? Is her decision self-serving?

Was Josh's decision to defer discussion of Lynn's recommendation respectful to Lynn, given the circumstances he was faced with? Why or why not?

In your career, have you ever been faced with a circumstance in which you are overwhelmed with a feeling of self-interest, as opposed to promoting the common good?

Is Dr. Frost's recommendation to go ahead with the project, based on the economic impact on Differencia and its employees, justifiable?

Is Mr. Finkelstein's directive to Josh to weigh all perspectives, in making the go-ahead decision, a reasonable one?

Is Dr. Gibson's decision to support bringing the Parkinson's drug to market, because of her family's connection to it, justifiable? Is self-interest justified here?

Mr. Finkelstein commands Josh to report back to the Board within one week, as to how to proceed. Is this a reasonable demand?

Dr. Foster asserts that the FDA drug approval process could take 10 to 15 years. Do you think that this is a reasonable amount of time to delay introduction of a drug that could have immediate lifesaving benefits?

Given that Lynn knew that the Parkinson's drug was ready for approval, was her initial decision to delay introduction of the drug justifiable?

Do you believe in situational ethics, i.e., acting in a way that contradicts action solely on the basis of moral principles instead of self -interest?

Key Leadership Qualities Identified

Magnanimity - Loftiness of spirit, enabling one to bear trouble calmly and proactively, so as to disdain meanness and to display a noble generosity, by providing resources to attack a problem instead of lamenting about one's plight.

Realistic Expectations - Setting goals and objectives based upon the likelihood that they can be achieved. It promotes goal achievement by creating a positive mindset in pursuing a goal.

Preemptive Concern for the Common Good - Exclusive dedication to a cause, which promotes the common good. Relentless pursuit of the common good in the face of obstacles. The goal of significant reduction in carbon emissions is an excellent example.

Opportunity Cost - What you must give up, buying what you want in terms of other goods and services. There is a high opportunity cost to spending money on consumer goods,, as opposed to research to develop drugs for life- threatening illnesses.

Situational Ethics - A theory where the situation is considered first, before deciding on the rules of right and wrong. There is no set of rules because what might be considered immoral in one situation could be considered the most moral thing to do in another. An example is if one believes in the absolute wrongness of abortion, then abortion could be morally acceptable based upon the situation.

Chapter 18
Josh and Lynn Nominated to Speak
at Pharmaceutical Convention

It is Thursday, June 16th, about 8:00 PM. I've had such a long day at work and feel exhausted. I am thinking about going home, having a late dinner with Lynn, and checking on my princess, Jessica, who will probably be sound asleep by the time I get home.

It is almost 9:00. I finally open the front door to my townhouse and put down my briefcase. I am soaking wet, wearing only a suit jacket without an umbrella, plus no hat. Lynn smiles at me and tells me to get comfortable She has prepared my favorite: baked lasagna, with a tall glass of Chardonnay. What else could I ask for?

Lynn asks me typical questions over dinner. "Josh, how was your day at work? Anything unusual happening that I should know about?" I don't have so very much to say. I am exhausted and can only think of eating, taking a shower, and going to bed. Lynn suddenly becomes very quiet and keeps looking and smirking as she eats. I look up at her and shout, "What? Why are you looking at me so funny? Open your mouth and tell me what is on your mind." I say all of this while I'm smiling at her in a mocking-type fashion.

Lynn reaches under her left leg and brings to the table an envelope, mailed to her and me. The return address is from "The Los Angeles Convention Center." I think that this is some advertisement. I get a million of these at the corporate office. I am ready to chuck the mailer into the waste basket, and she grabs my hand. She looks at me with that same contentious stare she always gives me when I am about to do something stupid.

"Don't throw that away, Josh. Please read it carefully. It is an invitation to speak at the Pharmaceutical Convention on Corporate Leadership and Accountability. We are the featured speakers if we accept." I look up at Lynn as I eat my lasagna and say to her, "Is this some joke? Are you kidding me? Do you realize that this convention center holds up to 10,000 people? Pharmaceutical companies will be attending from all over the world at this convention. The date is stamped on this presentation. If we accept, our speech will be Tuesday, August 16th, from 9:00-11:30 PM, with refereed questions and answers on written cards. Hundreds of companies worldwide will be directly or indirectly represented at this convention."

I am getting very nervous now, and I realize the magnitude of participating in something massive. I checked the invitation, and it is authentic. Lynn and I started a new Company with Dr. Mulcahy. We created a new culture, a new way of thinking, and a path toward leadership authenticity. It was a painstaking road. Many sacrifices were made personally and professionally. Many obstacles needed to be overcome, and we persevered through the roughest storms and the mightiest of seas. Lynn and I had seen life and death before us, and realized that relationships were only as good as the core values of the individuals in those relationships.

We finish our supper and do what we always do. We clean the dishes, check on Jessica, and then go to the loveseat to have a quick coffee before bed. Lynn looks at me solemnly while we are having coffee. It is almost 10:00 PM, and it appears that the caffeine in the coffee is keeping me awake. My mind is spinning, and I am overwhelmed by what I have just read.

Lynn grabs my hand as she has done so many times before, when I know she's about to say something I do not truly like or agree with. I think we're getting close to that moment. "Josh, you know about my medical condition. I fear this type of stress might set me back, by the end of my six-month assessment in October. I really can't risk this right now. I need to be ready to go back to work and help you run this wonderful company that we started, especially now that the Parkinson's drug is on its way to being cleared for full approval, and ready to hit the market for consumption way ahead of our competitors."

My response to Lynn is sincere. However, it is sheepish. "Lynn, we have been through everything together, and I don't know how I can get in front of thousands of people and make this presentation by myself. I need you up there with me. I don't know if I can pull this off myself. I mean, do I have to go? I don't have to do this. Maybe Dr. Mulcahy can go in my place. After all, she is the one that helped us begin Differencia."

Lynn is saddened by my response and pulls her hands back from mine. She looks away from me as I watch her face reddening and tears beginning to flow from her eyes, as she shakes her head slowly, back and forth. Lynn grabs some tissues from the coffee table in front of the loveseat, wipes her eyes, and looks me squarely in the face.

"Josh, I am at a loss for words right now, to respond to what you just said to me. Everything we have been through together, starting in 2013, from when I first met you, has blown up in my face. I don't know whether to be angry, sad, disappointed, or just plain disgusted right now." I interrupt Lynn, and she abruptly says, "Let me finish!" I could see the fire in her eyes and the determination in her voice, of what she is about to tell me.

"Josh, you are so self-centered, as you have been since I've known you over the past decade. You can't be mentored or taught anything that invades your circle, and you would prefer to throw me under the bus to save your hide. You don't care about Differencia, nor do you care about Jessica or me. You only care about protecting that fragile ego, and would even throw yourself under the bus to preserve anyone knowing the real you."

I feel the blood rushing to my head. My hands are getting cold and clammy, and the room is beginning to spin, signaling another anxiety attack. Is Lynn telling me the truth about who I am? I don't know what she's talking about. I am not trying to hide or preserve anything. I don't even know this person that just spoke out, who I thought was my wife, life partner, mother of my child, my best friend. Everything around me seems to separate from my existence. Lynn just attacked the core of my soul, and I will not sit here and take this from her. I don't care how this affects her. How can she say that I don't care about my child? I love Jessica more than my life. I'm not going to sit idly and let her make these accusations!

"Lynn, what you just said to me put a hole into my soul. How dare you say those horrible things to me, after we have been in a relationship for almost a decade. My ego has been and remains strong. I have fought for you tooth and nail. I protected our daughter and saw after her when we thought you were missing and then possibly died because of an aneurysm. I battled with myself and took strides I never thought I could take, to protect you and our daughter."

Lynn is ready to respond, and this time, I'm saying to her, "Let me finish." Lynn gets up from the loveseat, goes to the refrigerator, and gets some ice water to cool her parched lips. She returns to the loveseat and, this time sits up, not facing me with her arms folded. Her demeanor remains very staunch. She appears angrier at my words than offended by them.

"My dear wife, mother of my child, business partner (Co-CEO), and Board member. Shall we add more titles to our relationship? You always seem to have the answers and always judge me. You question my ability to lead. I have proven to you time and time again that I can get things done. I just happen to do them a little bit differently than you. I have more compassion than you could ever have, for this family and our company. You are so disconnected. Maybe, the reason is that you want to protect your fragile ego!"

Lynn gasps at my accusations. This time, she turns toward me and faces me. "Josh, I am not going to rebut your comments." Her words were calm yet focused. She is speaking in a very monotone manner, quite softly. "Josh, what we just did to each other is often what compelling leaders do in business, government, and family life." She grabs more tissues as the tears are streaming from her eyes. "Neither of us have fragile egos. However, when we attack each other in this manner, we destroy each other. This behavior is generated from us taking sides, to protect ourselves from harm. It is a human instinct."

Lynn grabs my hands once again and massages the palms of my hands with her thumbs very tenderly and continues. "Josh, we are leaders in one of the most powerful pharmaceutical companies in the world. We created a new Company to help those afflicted with diseases, that would otherwise die, without the drugs we create. Let's not make this about us. Let's talk about what we can do together more than what we can do separately."

I look at Lynn, chuckle, and shake my head. "Lynn, I realize what you're saying to me is all about authentic leadership. It is taking the 'I' out of the equation and putting in the 'we.' She smiles at me and says, "I love you, Josh, with all my heart and soul. I would never put you in a position that would hurt or jeopardize our family or Company. I chose not to attend this pharmaceutical convention because I want to be there with you, when I am hopefully cleared to come back to work. If you choose not to go to this convention alone, how will I ever know whether you can run Differencia as its CEO, if I can't return to work because of my illness?"

My response to Lynn is simple and to the point. "Who nominated me and you to make this presentation as its guest speakers?" Lynn looks at me and smiles. "Dr. Marcia Gibson, Board member. Remember her, Josh?"

Chapter 18
Lessons Learned

Josh arrives home at 9:00 PM to have dinner with Lynn and Jessica.

Lynn opens an envelope mailed to her from the Los Angeles Convention Center. It is an invitation to speak at the Pharmaceutical Convention on Corporate Leadership and Accountability.

Josh asserts that hundreds of companies worldwide will be attending the Convention. He realizes the importance of making a stellar presentation to improve Differencia's brand.

Lynn tells Josh that she is reluctant to make the presentation, as she fears the stress will set her recovery back.

Josh worries that he cannot make the presentation by himself. He suggests that Dr. Mulcahy could go in this place.

Lynn accuses Josh of being self-centered, and that he is only concerned with protecting his ego from being damaged.

Josh considers if what Lynn said is true. He expresses his anger on being accused of not dedicating his life to her and Jessica. He resents her doubt about his ability to lead. He tells Lynn that he has more compassion than her for their family and Differencia, and that she is trying to preserve her ego.

Lynn indicates that their contentious dialogue is typical of what businesses, government, and family members do every day to protect their egos.

Lynn states that their focus should be on making Differencia a successful pharmaceutical company, which will develop lifesaving drugs for the public

Based upon their conversation, Lynn indicates that she does not want to put Josh in a position to jeopardize their family or Differencia. She states that she does not want to attend the Convention, so that she can be cleared to return to work. She asks Josh that if he chooses not to attend the Convention, how will she know he can run Differencia as CEO alone.

Lynn states that Dr. Marcia Gibson nominated her and Josh to make the presentation at the Convention.

Questions to Ponder

Is Josh correct in his perception that the Convention presentation is extremely important in establishing the Differencia brand? Is he overreacting? Have you ever faced a similar situation in your career?

Is Lynn's decision to not make the presentation an overreaction on her part? Is she being too cautious? Have you faced a similar situation in your career?

Is Josh exhibiting leadership weakness when he suggests that Dr. Mulcahy should make the presentation? Have you ever been criticized for being overly concerned with preserving your ego?

Is Lynn's decision to not make the presentation an over-reaction on her part? Is she being too cautious?

Do you agree with Lynn's assertion that Josh is self-centered and is only concerned with protecting his fragile ego?

Do you agree with Josh's resentment of Lynn's doubt in his ability to lead, and her belief that she has more compassion than him about family life and Differencia?

Do you believe that the dialogue between Lynn and Josh is commonplace in everyday life? Have you ever had this dialogue with a significant other or others in your life?

In your view, is the relationship between Josh and Lynn deteriorating? If so, how can this relationship be improved?

Key Leadership Qualities Identified

Ego - Self-esteem. Not giving up easily in any contest or competition. Having confidence in one's ability to pursue and achieve a goal. This is important in developing a positive mind set.

Brand - A public image, reputation, or identity conceived of as something to be marketed or promoted. Authentic Leaders develop a distinct brand for the products and services of their organization. General Electric has always been known for its product innovations.

Equanimity - Evenness of mind, especially under stress. Not overreacting to immediate circumstances or crises. Abraham Lincoln reacted to Civil War crises with a calm demeanor and thoughtfulness.

Confidence in Others - Delegating tasks to others and empowering them to achieve desired goals. Strong leaders set goals and allow others to pursue these goals in their own way. Effective leaders provide others with the resources needed to accomplish goals.

Introspection - A reflective looking inward. An examination of one's own thoughts and feelings. This is necessary for self-improvement. By analyzing the results of past actions, one is able to improve decision-making.

Chapter 19
Josh Keating to Speak at Pharmaceutical Convention

It is Monday, August 15th, the day before my presentation at the pharmaceutical convention. I'll be speaking between 9:00 and 11:30 AM. I am very nervous and can't believe I'll be speaking to an industry whose total value exceeds $625 billion, or approximately 3.2% of the US gross domestic product.

I don't know how I got to where I am right now, representing one of the largest pharmaceutical companies in the world, that I helped put together with the love of my life, Dr. Lynn Ann Marconi. Together, we developed a strategic plan with an upright and prominent scientist, Dr. Bonnie Mulcahy. I was part of that, and for many reasons, I can rationalize why I don't deserve to be on this team.

I have flaunted many of my responsibilities throughout my career, spanning over twenty-five years as an accountant, then an account executive working for two major companies. I am one out of hundreds of thousands of individuals in this industry, who work for hundreds of companies around the world that are publicly traded. Some are still privately owned.

I'm trying to rationalize that I deserve this distinction. Lynn says I do. Bonnie Mulcahy nominated Lynn and me to make the speech on "Corporate Leadership and Accountability." What can I tell these global giants that they don't already know? What are we doing differently in leadership that is more effective than how they run their companies?

I have prepared my speech and am as ready as I'll ever be. Sometimes, leaders need to take risks. Things aren't always the way that they appear. I know that firsthand, on so many levels, beginning on that dreadful day of August 2nd, 2021, when my whole world started to crumble in less than a week, and it was just Jessica and me against the world. The love of my life was missing from my life, and I didn't know how to find her. When I finally found her, she was on the verge of getting brain surgery and fighting for her life. It was just Jessica and me.

I learned so much about my daughter, and she learned things about her Daddy that she never knew. I learned that leadership, that is, authentic leadership, is not about going into a company, sitting behind a desk in a plush office chair, and looking at a panoramic view outside your office window. All your soldiers fall into place to receive your orders for the day. It would help if you learned these things the hard way. It would help if you were mentored. You must mentor others to get to the top. However, you don't always have to get to the top of anything. It would help if you got to the bottom of what makes you tick first, before getting others motivated to see your vision.

Well, enough about me. I am a little hungry, and Jessica has the day off from school today. They are renovating her school building. California has stringent laws regulating environmental conditions on buildings under construction. At any rate, Jessica is up and comes into the kitchen as I go over my notes for my speech tomorrow. I must arrive early at the convention center, around 7:00 AM, to get set up. I need to make sure the lighting is proper, and my PowerPoint slides are in place. All the items on the agenda for the day need to be coordinated and lined up, so that the master of ceremonies can adequately introduce all of the lectures and seminars going on for the next three days, after tomorrow's opening of the convention.

It is not that I am ignoring Jessica, but I am so into my notes that I don't see her just standing in front of me, making gestures toward her tummy, telling me in no uncertain terms that she is hungry. It is 7:00 AM, Mommy is still sleeping, and she knows I have taken the day off to prepare for tomorrow.

I look up at Jessica and say to her very snidely, "What can I do for a very hungry six-year-old this morning?" She looks up at me with her big bluish-green eyes. "Let's go out for breakfast, Daddy?" I respond, "I don't think I have any money, little girl." She runs up to me, sits on my lap, and stares at me without saying a word. She is just such a beautiful little girl, inside and out, and has taught me so much about myself, especially when Lynn was sick, and we didn't know if she would make it.

Oh God, I need Jessica's strength right now. As it gets closer to my presentation tomorrow, I am getting nervous, and the butterflies are consuming my stomach to the point where I feel nauseous. Out of the blue, she puts her tiny hand inside my hand and stares at me, as if she was looking right through into my soul. "Daddy, do you remember when Mommy was sick, and we didn't know if she was going to die?" I respond, "Yes, of course, sweetheart. Why would you ask me this now?" She takes her hand out of my hand, folds her arms, and starts rocking back and forth like she usually does when she gets fixated on a topic.

I am somewhat at a loss for words, as I don't know what this child is talking about, and why she is making the connection to that horrible time back in the hospital over a year ago. "Daddy, Mommy needed you to pray for her. You knew that Daddy. We prayed together." The tears start falling from Jessica's face, and she grabs my hand and squeezes it real hard. "Mommy told me you were going to talk about something big tomorrow. I asked her what you were going to talk about. She told me it was about being a leader. Daddy, are you my leader? What does that mean?"

I didn't realize that Lynn was watching our conversation, as she had already awakened and was ready to pour herself a glass of juice, as she always does every morning. She just stood there and listened to Jessica and me have this conversation. I knew Lynn was standing at the threshold of the kitchen. However, Jessica's back was facing her, and she could not see her mother watching and observing.

"Jessica, I am a leader. I am a real leader. I am not somebody who tells other people what to do. I was leading in the hospital when I talked to you about Mommy. I was leading when I talked to Dr. Pereira about what to do when she was very sick. I had to decide on important stuff, to save Mommy's life or end it. Do you understand?" Jessica responds. "Yes, Daddy, I do understand. You were leading me when you told me to pray for Mommy. You were leading me when you explained why God made that little girl die in the hospital that had Covid."

"Jessica, God didn't make that little girl die. Do you mean this??? We couldn't save her with the medicine that we had. God gives us the tools to make people better; that is what our Company does. We make drugs that make people better. God gives us the wisdom to use our brains to make us live longer. I am proud to be part of that. You see, Jessica, real leadership means making sacrifices, sometimes even putting your life in danger to save the lives of others. It means standing up for the truth. The most important thing, Jessica, is that we are all connected. Everybody in this world is connected."

I see that Jessica takes all of this in; the meaning of leadership absorbs her. This is what I'm going to be talking about tomorrow. If I cut it, I will be happy. If there is a warm reception to what I am saying, that will be good. If my presentation is not well received, I will do better next time. This is what leaders do. When they fall, they get up, wipe themselves off, and try again until they get it right. However, I now realize that what differentiates leaders from managers is that leaders set their bars high, but never boast perfection. They are on a continuing journey of improvement.

Jessica looks at me and says, "Daddy, did the prayers make Mommy better? Or did the doctors make Mommy better?" I don't know how to respond to this child. At this point, Lynn decides that she is going to chime in. Jessica jumps off my lap, runs to her mother, and sits on her lap. She is acting like a typical six-year-old, rather than a genius protege.

Lynn says to me, "Josh, do you mind if I answer Jessica's question, the one that you just asked her about God and the doctors?" I tell Lynn to be my guest. "Jessica, the power of prayer is special to so many people. Prayer has been important to everyone on this planet for many different reasons. Many people believe in many different things. However, prayer is a way to say that somebody is always looking after us. We are all connected. This is what makes us human. Do you understand what I mean, Jessica?"

Jessica responds, "Mommy, do leaders need prayers?" Lynn responds, "Jessica, everybody needs prayers. When mommy was very sick, I held your hand and heard your voice even though I was sleeping in a coma. I heard Daddy's voice. The truth is, I can't explain it, but your prayers helped me get better. The wonderful doctors in the hospital helped me get better. You see, our connection to each other makes us get better. When we fall, we get up and start again. We never quit."

Jessica is staring at me most intensely while on Lynn's lap. Finally, she says, "Daddy is going to make a speech tomorrow. I know you can't be with him, Mommy. Do you think he'll do okay?" I look at Jessica and wink while she is still sitting on her Mommy's lap. Lynn responds. "I will be with him in spirit and pray for him as he prayed for me. Your Daddy is a leader, Jessica. This is why he can do the speech tomorrow; I don't have to be with him. He will do just fine!"

It is August 16th, and I am at the LA convention center at 7:00 AM sharp. I check out all the equipment and the large main dining room, which is 36,242 square feet and can accommodate up to 2,700 people without any divided spaces. This is the room that I am going to be speaking in. I am so overwhelmed by its size. There are many large-screen monitors, and my speech will be streamed around the world through the pharma 1000 network by my surroundings. It makes me dizzy to look at this vast complex. The parking lot accommodates up to 5,600 cars. I will be positioned on a huge circular stage in the center of my audience.

It is 7:30 AM. I grab a coffee and a danish. I am conversing with the events director, a makeup artist doing my face over while talking to the director, and a program manager introducing me to the sound manager. This is so wild that I am getting all this attention. However, I am sure all these steps are necessary before proceeding. What is remarkable about all of this is that I sent them my speech ahead of time through an email, and it's already on the monitor, ready for me to read as I deliver my speech.

My speech is only about twenty minutes long. However, the opening ceremonies, reviewing the main events and the workshops, including late registrations, will take about thirty-five minutes. Although they state that I will be on from 9:00 AM to 11:30 AM, the reality of the situation is that I will only be speaking between 10:00 AM and 10:25 AM. There will be a fifteen-minute question and answer session, which will bring us to approximately 10:50 AM, including interruptions. Then, they will take a thirty-minute break to network. This will get us to about 11:30, give or take. The rest of the time will be workshops developed around my speech this morning. I will go from table to table, make comments, and mentor. Of those that are participating in the workshops, many of them include pharmaceutical companies competing with us. All in all, I think this is all nice.

It is 9:00 AM, and this is my moment in time. Once introduced, I approach the stage and feel Jessica and Lynn beside me, supporting me. I think it is prayers they are sending me. I am not alone. I am connected to some of the best people on the planet. These people research, develop and make pharmaceutical products that help save lives. Our competition makes us competitive to come up with the best solutions to the worst problems that affect our quality of life every day. I am asking you, my readers, not to be judgmental and to be open-minded, as I am about to reiterate to this massive group of people the same goals that are in my mind. Let's leave the world a little better than we found after entering it.

"Dear Pharmaceutical Colleagues, my name is Joshua Keating. Dr. Lynn Ann Marconi and I are truly honored to have been nominated and selected as featured speakers for today's opening session of our

pharmaceutical convention. Dr. Marconi regrets that she cannot attend today, as she has been ironing out some medical issues, which are non-life-threatening at this point. She is working with me in total capacity as Co-CEO of our newly formed Company, Differencia.

Dr. Marconi and I both understand that our nomination was based on a recommendation by the Board Director of Differencia, Dr. Bonnie Mulcahy. Dr. Mulcahy, Dr. Marconi, and I have worked feverishly over the last thirteen months to transition Medical Solutions, Inc. to what is now known as Differencia. We believed forming this new Company would leave Medical Solutions behind, and build a new enterprise whose goal is to reassess our core values, rewrite a mission statement, and abide by a vision set forth by the founders of Medical Solutions almost 40 years ago.

It is no secret and has been widely publicized that our transition team needed to include new Board members and stakeholders, to honor our core values that have precipitated our successes for many years. We are ready to go forward and align our sites on launching the new Parkinson's drug, for patients in the early stages of the disease, that may stop, slow down, or even eradicate Parkinson's from them altogether. Wouldn't this be amazing?

The FDA has completed our preliminary testing, and we are awaiting the final approval, no later than ten months from now. I just wanted to share this news with you before we get started. My speech is going to be simple and not exhaustive. I am here to talk to you about Authentic

Leadership and Sustainability. You might ask why the talk I present today is not about Corporate Leadership, but Authentic Leadership.

This is not a play on words. Authentic Leadership does not just involve corporate leadership. It requires application in the home, in the hospital, and the playground, or in any other setting that you can think of where supervision is required.

Ladies and gentlemen, leadership starts with you. You need to discover the leader within yourself, and define your Leadership Gene so that you can use it, embellish upon it, and continue to grow it until you become The Authentic Leader.

I have learned the hard way that leadership isn't easy. Management is structured and follows a strict set of protocols. Leaders find out the hard way that protocols, although necessary, do not always provide the best paths to solving problems. It takes courage, hope, stamina, and finally, determination.

When it appears that your world is floundering around you, and you are losing sight of where you are and where your fiduciary responsibilities lie, you must often depend on your instincts to make decisions that you know in your heart are right.

A year ago, I thought I had lost my then-life partner and now my wife, Dr. Marconi. When we first met, we had no intention of becoming intimately involved. We did not choose this path. Instead, it chose us. We were determined to balance work and personal life. We had a beautiful child together and gave this child the name Jessica. She is our legacy.

At the same time, we were planning a new Company with a vision that was never brought to fruition with Medical Solutions. The founders of Medical Solutions wrote a beautiful vision statement, and we kept it. That vision reflected our core values. It was about more than what we did; it reflected who we are. You can't have one without the other. It would help if you integrated both things. We need to identify what type of leaders we are and want to be going forward in our profession.

Our job is to change lives through our medicines. They give hope to people who would otherwise have no hope. There is no amount of money you can put on any type of drug we manufacture that saves lives.

A year ago, it was the doctors at the LA Medical Center that found a way to correctly identify Lynn's illness, so that she could be with us today. I can't imagine what it must be like, to have others experience what I experienced. On the same token, I can't possibly fathom what it feels like to lose someone you knew you maybe could save, but didn't have the medicine to cure.

Raising money is an essential part of how we keep ourselves alive. We need benefactors. We need endowments and researchers to find the resources to support us and keep our businesses afloat, so that we can continue to do what we do best.

Leadership is not easy. Authentic leadership is even more challenging. It would help if people saw the broader spectrum of leading, in a world that often misinterprets the value of medicine. Many individuals have no idea how talented our staff is. These people work day in and day out to find cures for incurable diseases.

I recently doubted my abilities to make a difference. I had a habit of pointing the finger at everyone else, when I made a mistake. I never blamed myself. It was always somebody else's fault. I had many good mentors in my life. Some of them passed on, and some remain. The words keep reverberating in my head. I have had good leaders, and I have had bad leaders. I learned from both. The good leaders taught me many beautiful things. The bad leaders taught me what not to do, how to fail, and why I should not mimic their ways.

If you want to look at sustainability, look to your left and right. Shake the hand of the person to your right, then look to your left and do the same. Whether they are your competitors or not, learn from them. Take good notes and continue to make a difference, leaving the world a little better than you found it. If you fall, get up, wipe yourself off, and don't ever quit until you succeed. This is what Authentic Leadership is all about. Our Company is Differencia, meaning "to make a difference."

Once you make that difference, you will become "The Authentic Leader." Until we meet again, this is Josh Keating signing off.

Chapter 19
Lessons Learned

Josh prepares for his presentation to the pharmaceutical convention the next day. He reflects on the reality that along with Lynn and Dr. Mulcahy, he has developed a strategic plan for Differencia.

In his preparation, Josh recollects Lynn's aneurysm, the cancellation of the Parkinson's drug announcement, the firing of him and Lynn, and the reinstating of Lynn as CEO, after Dr Fringe's firing, because of her intent to provide falsified data to the FDA.

Josh reviews his notes for the presentation and focuses on the logistics for the meeting.

Upon interacting with Josh, Jessica asks him if he is a leader, and asks him what it means to be a leader.

Josh tells Jessica that he is a real leader. She responds by saying that Josh was leading when he explained why God made Mary Ann Taylor Norton die in the hospital.

Real leadership means making sacrifices, even if it involves putting your life in danger, to promote the common good.

Josh muses is that if the presentation does not go well, he will do better the next time. Leaders constantly strive to improve themselves.

Lynn answers Jessica's question by saying that praying is the act of talking with God. People pray to ask God to help them face challenges they are experiencing.

Lynn tells Jessica that leaders need prayers to accomplish their goals. It helps them to be resilient and never quit.

Jessica asks Lynn if Josh will be able to make the convention presentation effectively. Lynn tells her that with the power of prayer, Josh will do just fine.

The presentation room is gigantic in size – 36,242 square feet, and can accommodate 2,700 people. Josh will be positioned on a significant stage facing the center of the audience.

The theme of Josh's speech is that Differencia's mission is to make the world a better place.

Josh begins his presentation and tells the audience that he regrets that Lynn cannot be there because of non-life-threatening medical issues. He indicates the nomination for Lynn and him to speak was based upon the recommendation of Differencia's Board Director, Dr. Bonnie Mulcahy.

Josh reports that the new Company will leave Medical Solutions behind, and build a new company whose goal will be to reassess its core values, rewrite a mission statement, and pursue a new vision set forth by the founders of Medical Solutions.

The FDA has completed preliminary testing, and Differencia is awaiting final approval from the FDA within 10 months.

Authentic leadership is distinct from corporate leadership, in that it involves individual leadership. It begins with the leadership genes each individual has within themselves, and requires self-improvement to successfully face challenges.

Josh reflects that he has made great mistakes, but seldom took responsibility for them. He has had good and bad leaders, and has learned from both of them.

Sustainability requires being connected to others and recognizing that we must work together to address issues affecting the public good. This will be the mission of the new Company, Differencia.

Questions to Ponder

Is Josh overthinking in his preparation for his presentation? Why or why not? Do you sometimes overprepare for presentations? Does this make you nervous?

Does Josh ruminate excessively about the past? Is this productive? Do you obsess about the past? What effect does this have on you?

Is Josh's response to Jessica on being a real leader a good one? Would you have answered differently?

Do you agree with Lynn's answer to Jessica of the role of prayer in leadership? Is prayer a practice you follow in making decisions and facing challenges?

Does Josh make an effective presentation to the convention audience?

How could it be improved? What would you have done differently?

Are you in agreement with Josh's distinction between corporate leadership and individual leadership? What are you more focused on in your life? Should you realign your focus?

Have Josh and Lynn done a good job in balancing the tradeoff between corporate and individual leadership?

Has Josh done an effective job in making the case to the audience that all of us must contribute resources to fund the creation of life-saving drugs at an affordable cost to the public?

Has Josh taken responsibility for the mistakes he has made in his personal and professional lives? Have you taken responsibility for mistakes that you have made?

What are the key factors affecting an organization's sustainability? Does your organization have a plan to promote its sustainability overtime?

Are you excited about following the character development of Josh, Lynn, and Jessica? As the storyline unfolds, would you be inclined to read the follow up book to Differencia?

Key Leadership Qualities Identified

Minimize Rumination - Rumination is to go over in the mind repeatedly. This leads to mental stress, a negative outlook, and poor decision-making. It often reflects agonizing over past failures.

Critical Reflection - A thought, idea, or opinion formed as a result of meditation. It allows one to think about the results of past actions, and apply the lessons learned to inform future actions.

Individual Leadership - Leadership which pursues the attainment of both personal and organizational goals. President Theodore Roosevelt overcame many obstacles in his life. In addition to growing stronger, he also worked toward eliminating corruption in the Police Department of New York City in the 1880s.

Prayer - An earnest request or wish to a higher being. The authentic leader believes that he is guided by a higher being. He believes that he does not have to "go it alone". This allows the leader to focus on what he can control, and leave the outcome in the hands of the higher being.

Business Development - Securing the resources necessary to achieve a goal. Successful leaders are able to convince others to give them funding to accomplish their goals. Benjamin Franklin was able to persuade France to provide him with funds to assist the colonists in battling the British Empire, which led to American Independence.

Accountability - An obligation to accept responsibility for or to account for one's actions. True leaders live with the consequences of their decisions and address those consequences. Abraham Lincoln made a promise to the American people that he would save the Union by abolishing slavery. He did this with the realization that his life would be in danger.

Vision - The thought, concept, or object formed by the imagination. It is a focus on what can be. President Kennedy had a vision that the US could land a man on the moon by the end of the 1960s. Through relentless efforts, a vision often becomes a reality.

Bibliography

"Leadership is a Choice." John DiCicco and Kenneth E. Strong, Jr., 2017.

"The Leadership Gene," John DiCicco, 2017.

"Our Nurturing Love Through the Silence," John DiCicco, 2011.

"On Air: My 50 Year Love Affair with Radio," Jordan Rich, 2021.

"Dare to Own You." Liz Bruner, 2021.

"The Seven Habits of Highly Effective People," Jim Collins, 2001.

"How to Win Friends and Influence People," Dale Carnegie, 1998.

"Talking to Strangers," Malcolm Gladwell, 2019.

"Outliers," Malcolm Gladwell, 2019.

"David and Goliath," Malcolm Gladwell, 2006.

"The Splendid and the Vile," Eric Larson, 2022.

"Truman," David McCullough, 1993.

"The Gift of Forgiveness," Katherine Schwarzenegger, 2020.

"Team of Rivals," Doris Kearns Goodwin, 2006.

"It's All About the Guest," Steve DeFilippo, 2013.

"Good to Great," Jim Collins, 2001.

"The Autobiography of Eleanor Roosevelt," Eleanor Roosevelt, 2014.

"The One Minute Manager," Ken Blanchard, 2003.

"Shouting at Leaves," Jennifer Mumba, 2021.

"The Wisdom of Crowds," James Surowiecki, 2005.

"The Trophy Kids Grow Up," Ron Alsop, 2008.

"Maximizing Cash Flow - The Path to Prosperity," Bruce J. Share, 2021.

"Tuesdays with Morrie," Mitch Albom, 2017.

"Eleanor," David Michaelis, 2021.

"Faith Still Moves Mountains," Harris Faulkner, 2022

"A Farewell to Arms," Ernest Hemingway, 2014.

"The Autobiography of Benjamin Franklin," 1791.

"Profiles in Courage," John F. Kennedy, 2006.

"The Biography of Abraham Lincoln," University Press, 2022.

"The Organization Man," William H. Whyte